莎士比亚

经典戏剧系列

罗密欧与朱丽叶

〔英〕莎士比亚 ◎ 著
朱生豪 ◎ 译

汉英对照

石油工业出版社

图书在版编目（CIP）数据

罗密欧与朱丽叶：汉英对照 /（英）莎士比亚著；朱生豪译 . —北京：石油工业出版社，2022.3
（莎士比亚经典戏剧系列）
ISBN 978-7-5183-4549-6

Ⅰ.①罗… Ⅱ.①莎…②朱… Ⅲ.①英语-汉语-对照读物②悲剧-剧本-英国-中世纪 Ⅳ.
①H319.4：Ⅰ

中国版本图书馆CIP数据核字（2021）第035112号

莎士比亚经典戏剧系列：罗密欧与朱丽叶（汉英对照）
〔英〕莎士比亚 著 朱生豪 译

出版发行：石油工业出版社
　　　　　（北京市朝阳区安华里二区1号楼　100011）
网　　　址：www.petropub.com
编 辑 部：（010）64523684
图书营销中心：（010）64523633
经　　销：全国新华书店
印　　刷：金世嘉元（唐山）印务有限公司

2022年3月第1版　　2022年3月第1次印刷
880毫米×1230毫米　　开本：1/32　　印张：8
字数：240千字

定价：45.00元
（如发现印装质量问题，我社图书营销中心负责调换）
版权所有，侵权必究

前　言

莎士比亚，一个辉映世界文学史的名字；莎士比亚戏剧，世界文学史上永恒的经典，引无数后来者阅读、膜拜。为了满足广大读者对莎士比亚作品孜孜不倦的追求，我们推出了这套"莎士比亚经典戏剧系列"丛书，精选十二部具有代表性的作品，包括四大悲剧、四大喜剧，以及其他四部不容错过的经典戏剧作品，以中英文对照的方式，呈现给读者朋友们。

英国前首相丘吉尔曾说："我宁愿失去一个印度，也不愿失去一个莎士比亚。"莎士比亚（1564—1616），英国文艺复兴时期伟大的剧作家，一生写下了154首十四行诗、2首长诗以及38部戏剧，被誉为"人类文学奥林匹斯山上的宙斯"。

尽管莎士比亚逝世已有四百多年，他的作品至今依旧脍炙人口。正如当初与他同时代的英国诗人本·琼森所称赞："他不属于一个时代而属于所有的世纪。"但是，作为一个生活在21世纪的中国的普通人，我们为什么要读莎士比亚呢？

除了其戏剧荡气回肠的语言、穿透人性的哲理，莎士比亚已经成为一个文化符号，其作品已成为与古希腊神话、《圣经》并列的西方文化母体之一。了解莎士比亚戏剧，是我们理解西方文化的一个重要途径。

即使没有读过莎士比亚的作品，我们也都听说过这句话：一千个读者，就有一千个哈姆莱特。莎士比亚作品中最具代表性的便是四大悲剧——《哈姆莱特》《奥赛罗》《李尔王》《麦克白》。《哈姆莱特》是对人的原罪的追溯，《奥赛罗》让我们明白人心实在是经不起试探，《李尔王》揭示了伦理道德的困惑，《麦克白》使我们见识了命运对人类的玩弄。这四大悲剧，描写的无论是怒火如仇的复仇、穷凶极恶的罪行，还是缠绵悱恻的爱情、野心勃勃的宫斗，都极富哲理，句句锥心，让人难以释怀。

喜剧在莎士比亚戏剧创作中也占有相当分量，莎士比亚四大喜剧包括《仲夏夜之梦》《威尼斯商人》《第十二夜》《皆大欢喜》，这些作品以机智风趣的语言将浪漫、抒情、讽刺的风格发挥得淋漓尽致，戏谑当中渗透着些许悲剧意味，更显其喜，蕴含着人文主义者的美好理想，以及对人类光明前途的展望。《仲夏夜之梦》讲述的是有情人终成眷属的故事，《威尼斯商人》成功地塑造了唯利是图的四大吝啬鬼形象之一——夏洛克，《第十二夜》赞美了爱情自由和个性解放，《皆大欢喜》反映了莎士比亚理想中的以善胜恶的美好境界。

除了四大悲剧与四大喜剧，莎士比亚的经典剧目还有《罗密欧与朱丽叶》《温莎的风流娘儿们》《雅典的泰门》《无事生非》。《罗密欧与朱丽叶》讲述了意大利贵族凯普莱特女儿朱丽叶与蒙太古的儿子罗密欧诚挚相爱，誓言相依，但因两家世代为仇而受到阻挠的故事，《温莎的风流娘儿们》是唯一一部以英国现实为背景反映市民生活的剧本，《雅典的泰门》揭露了拜金主义的罪恶，《无事生非》围绕爱情主题并行两条线索，诠释了美好的爱情。

俄国评论家别林斯基说："他（莎士比亚）的每一个剧本都是一个世界的缩影，包含着整个现在、过去及未来。"时至今日，我们仍然能在这四百年前的戏剧中，看到自己的影子。如果你有书架，你一定要摆放一套莎士比亚,因为你几乎所有的人生困惑,莎士比亚都有解药。读莎士比亚,提高的不仅是你的文学素养,还有你的主观幸福感。

好的作品还要有好的翻译。朱生豪(1912—1944),浙江嘉兴人,从24岁起开始翻译莎士比亚作品,直至32岁病逝。他所翻译的莎剧,是公认最能显现莎剧神韵、最通俗易懂的译本,正如他自己所说:"余译此书之宗旨,第一在求于尽可能之范围内,保持原作之神韵;必不得已而求其次,亦必以明白晓畅之字句,忠实传达原文之意趣;而于逐字逐句对照式之硬译,则未敢赞同。"这套莎士比亚经典戏剧系列,即选用了朱生豪先生的译本,希望给您带来一场不同凡响的阅读旅程。

《罗密欧与朱丽叶》导读

《罗密欧与朱丽叶》是莎士比亚早期创作的一部悲剧,创作于1593—1594年间,讲述的是蒙太古之子罗密欧和凯普莱特之女朱丽叶一见钟情,为了追求自由的爱情,不顾家族的世仇,最终殉情的悲剧故事。

凯普莱特和蒙太古是古城维罗纳的两大家族,这两大家族有世仇,他们之间经常发生械斗。蒙太古家的儿子罗密欧,喜欢上了一个女孩罗瑟琳,当听说罗瑟琳要参加凯普莱特家的化装舞会后,他戴上面具,混进了宴会场。

但在这次宴会上,罗密欧对凯普莱特家的独生女儿朱丽叶一见钟情。当晚,美若天仙的朱丽叶是宴会的主角,罗密欧隐瞒自己的身份,上前向朱丽叶表达自己的爱慕之情,朱丽叶也对罗密欧颇有好感。当双方知道彼此的身份后,两人都为自己爱上仇家的儿女而感到不安。在凯普莱特家的花园,他们互诉衷肠,最后决定秘密成婚。

第二天,罗密欧去向修道院的神父求助。神父答应了罗密欧的请求,觉得这是化解两家矛盾的一个途径。罗密欧通过朱丽叶的乳母把朱丽叶约到了修道院,在神父的主持下二人结成夫妻。这天中午,罗密欧在街上遇到了朱丽叶的堂兄提伯尔特,他要和罗密欧决斗,罗密欧不愿决斗,罗密欧的朋友为他打抱不平,和提伯尔特展开了决斗,结果却被提伯尔特借机杀死。罗密欧大怒,拔剑为朋友报仇,杀死了提伯尔特。

经过多方协商,城市的统治者决定驱逐罗密欧,如果他敢回来就处死他。朱丽叶很伤心，罗密欧也不愿离开，在神父的劝说下他才同意暂时离开。这天晚上，他偷偷爬进朱丽叶的卧室，度过了新婚之夜。第二天天一亮，罗密欧就不得不开始了流放生活。罗密欧刚一离开，出身高贵的帕里斯伯爵前来向朱丽叶求婚。凯普莱特非常满意，命令朱丽叶三天后就结婚。

朱丽叶去找神父想办法，神父给了她一种药，这种药服下去后就像死了一样，但四十二小时后就会醒过来。神父答应她会派人通知罗密欧来挖开墓穴，之后她可以和罗密欧远走高飞。朱丽叶在婚礼的前一天晚上服了药，第二天婚礼变成了葬礼。神父马上派人去通知罗密欧。可是，罗密欧在这之前听说了葬礼的事情，他以为朱丽叶真的死了。他在半夜赶到了朱丽叶的墓穴旁，杀死了同一时间赶来的帕里斯伯爵，之后掘开墓穴，吻了一下朱丽叶，便掏出随身带来的毒药一饮而尽，倒在了朱丽叶身旁。朱丽叶醒来后见到死去的罗密欧，悲痛欲绝，她拔出罗密欧的剑刺向自己，倒在了罗密欧身上。神父和两大家族的人陆续赶来，神父向大家讲述了罗密欧和朱丽叶的故事。失去儿女的父母们如梦初醒。从此，两大家族消除积怨，并在城中为罗密欧和朱丽叶各铸了一座金像。

《罗密欧与朱丽叶》是莎士比亚悲剧中浪漫主义抒情色彩最浓的一部悲剧。朱生豪先生在翻译这部戏剧时曾评价："《罗密欧与朱丽叶》是莎士比亚早期的抒情悲剧，也是继《所罗门雅歌》之后最美丽悱恻的恋歌。这里并没有对人性进行深刻的解剖，只是真挚地道出了全世界青年男女的心声，爱情不但战胜了死亡，并且使两族的世仇消弭于无形；从这个意义上来看，它无疑是一本讴歌爱情至上的戏剧。"

译者自序

于世界文学史中，足以笼罩一世，凌越千古，卓然为词坛之宗匠，诗人之冠冕者，其唯希腊之荷马，意大利之但丁，英之莎士比亚，德之歌德乎。此四子者，各于其不同之时代及环境中，发为不朽之歌声。然荷马史诗中之英雄，既与吾人之现实生活相去过远，但丁之天堂地狱，复与近代思想诸多抵牾；歌德去吾人较近，彼实为近代精神之卓越的代表。然以超脱时空限制一点而论，则莎士比亚之成就，实远在三子之上。盖莎翁笔下之人物，虽多为古代之贵族阶级，然其所发掘者，实为古今中外贵贱贫富人人所同具之人性。故虽经三百余年以后，不仅其书为全世界文学之士所耽读，其剧本且在各国舞台与银幕上历久搬演而弗衰，盖由其作品中具有永久性与普遍性，故能深入人心如此耳。

中国读者耳莎翁大名已久，文坛知名之士，亦尝将其作品译出多种，然历观坊间各译本失之于粗疏草率者尚少，失之于拘泥生硬者实繁有徒。拘泥字句之结果，不仅原作神味，荡焉无存，甚至艰深晦涩，有若天书，令人不能卒读，此则译者之过，莎翁不能任其咎者也。

余笃嗜莎剧，尝首尾严诵全集至十余遍，于原作精神，自觉颇有会心。廿四年春，得前辈同事詹文浒先生之鼓励，始着手为翻译全集之尝试。越年战事发生，历年来辛苦搜集之各种莎集版本，及诸家注释考证批评之书，不下一二百册，悉数毁于炮火，仓卒中唯携出牛津版全集一册，及译稿数本而已。厥后转辗流徙，为生活而奔波，更无暇晷，以续未竟之志。及卅一年春，目睹事变日亟，闭户家居，摈绝外务，始得专心一志，致力译事。虽贫穷疾病，交相煎迫，而埋头伏案，握管不辍。凡前后历十年而全稿完成，夫以译莎工作之艰巨，十年之功，不可云久，然毕生精力，殆已尽注于兹矣。

余译此书之宗旨，第一在求最大可能之范围内，保持原作之神韵；必不得已而求其次，亦必以明白晓畅之字句，忠实传达原文之意趣；而于逐字逐句对照式之硬译，则未敢赞同。凡遇原文中与中国语法不合之处，往往再四咀嚼，不惜全部更易原文之结构，务使作者之命意豁然呈露，不为晦涩之字句所掩蔽。每译一段竟，必先自拟为读者，察阅译文中有无暧昧不明之处。又必自拟为舞台上之演员，审辨语调之是否顺口，音节之是否调和，一字一句之未惬，往往苦思累日。然才力所限，未能尽符理想；乡居僻陋，既无参考之书籍，又鲜质疑之师友。谬误之处，自知不免。所望海内学人，惠予纠正，幸甚幸甚！

生豪书于三十三年四月

Contents
目　录

DRAMATIS PERSONAE　/　2

剧中人物　/　3

Act I　/　8

第一幕　/　9

Act II　/　66

第二幕　/　67

Act III　/　116

第三幕　/　117

Act IV　/　178

第四幕　/　179

Act V　/　210

第五幕　/　211

DRAMATIS PERSONAE

ESCALUS Prince of Verona

PARIS a young Count, kinsman to the Prince

MONTAGUE
CAPULET } heads of two houses at variance with each other

ROMEO son to Montague

MERCUTIO kinsman to the Prince, and friend to Romeo

BENVOLIO nephew to Montague, and friend to Romeo

TYBALT nephew to Lady Capulet

FRIAR LAURENCE Franciscan

FRIAR JOHN Franciscan

BALTHASAR servant to Romeo

ABRAM servant to Montague

SAMPSON
GREGORY } servant to Capulet

PETER servant to Juliet's nurse

An Apothecary

Three Musicians

LADY MONTAGUE wife to Montague

LADY CAPULET wife to Capulet

剧中人物

爱斯卡勒斯　维罗纳亲王

帕　里　斯　少年贵族,亲王的亲戚

蒙　太　古 ⎫
凯　普　莱　特 ⎬ 互相敌视的两家家长

罗　密　欧　蒙太古之子

茂丘西奥　亲王的亲戚,罗密欧的朋友

班伏里奥　蒙太古之侄,罗密欧的朋友

提伯尔特　凯普莱特夫人之侄

劳伦斯神父　法兰西斯派教士

约翰神父　与劳伦斯同门的教士

鲍尔萨泽　罗密欧的仆人

亚伯拉罕　蒙太古的仆人

山　普　孙 ⎫
葛　莱　古　里 ⎬ 凯普莱特的仆人

彼　得　朱丽叶乳母的从仆

卖　药　人

乐　工　三　人

蒙太古夫人

凯普莱特夫人

JULIET *daughter to Capulet*

Nurse to Juliet

Citizens of Verona, Gentlemen and Gentlewomen of both houses, Maskers, Torchbearers, Pages, Guards, Watchmen, Servants, and Attendants

SCENE

Verona, Mantua

朱丽叶　　　　凯普莱特之女

朱丽叶的乳母

维罗纳市民；两家男女亲属；跳舞者、戴面具者、持火把者、听差、卫士、巡丁及侍从等致辞者

地　点

维罗纳，曼图亚

PROLOGUE

[*Enter Chorus.*]

Two households, both alike in dignity,

In fair Verona, where we lay our scene,

From ancient grudge break to new mutiny,

Where civil blood makes civil hands unclean.

From forth the fatal loins of these two foes

A pair of star-coss'd lovers take their life;

Whose misadventur'd piteous overthrows

Doth with their death bury their parents' strife.

The fearful passage of their death-mark'd love,

And the continuance of their parents' rage,

Which, but their children's end, naught could remove,

Is now the two hours' traffic of our stage;

The which if you with patient ears attend,

What here shall miss, our toil shall strive to mend.

[*Exit.*]

开场诗

（致辞者上念）

故事发生在维罗纳名城，
有两家门第相当的巨族，
累世的宿怨激起了新争，
鲜血把市民的白手污渎。
是命运注定这两家仇敌，
生下了一双不幸的恋人，
他们的悲惨凄凉的殒灭，
和解了他们交恶的尊亲。
这一段生生死死的恋爱，
还有那两家父母的嫌隙，
把一对多情的儿女杀害，
演成了今天这一本戏剧。
交代过这几句挈领提纲，
请诸位耐着心细听端详。（下）

Act I

SCENE I Verona. A public place.

[Enter Sampson and Gregory, with swords and bucklers, of the house of Capulet.]

SAMPSON   Gregory, on my word, we'll not carry coals.

GREGORY   No, for then we should be colliers.

SAMPSON   I mean, as we be in choler, we'll draw.

GREGORY   Ay, while you live, draw your neck out of collar.

SAMPSON   I strike quickly, being moved.

GREGORY   But thou art not quickly moved to strike.

SAMPSON   A dog of the house of Montague moves me.

GREGORY   To move is to stir, and to be valiant is to stand. Therefore, if thou art moved, thou runn'st away.

SAMPSON   A dog of that house shall move me to stand. I will take the wall of any man or maid of Montague's.

GREGORY   That shows thee a weak slave; for the weakest goes to the wall.

SAMPSON   'Tis true; and therefore women, being the weaker vessels, are ever thrust to the wall. Therefore I will push Montague's men from the wall and thrust his maids to the wall.

GREGORY   The quarrel is between our masters and us their men.

SAMPSON   'Tis all one. I will show myself a tyrant. When I have fought with the men, I will be civil with the maids — I will cut off their heads.

GREGORY   The heads of the maids?

第一幕

第一场　维罗纳。广场

（山普孙及葛莱古里各持盾剑上）

山 普 孙　葛莱古里，咱们可真的不能让人家当做苦力一样欺侮。
葛莱古里　对了，咱们不是可以随便给人欺侮的。
山 普 孙　我说，咱们要是发起脾气来，就会拔剑动武。
葛莱古里　对了，你可不要把脖子缩到领口里去。
山 普 孙　我一动性子，我的剑是不认人的。
葛莱古里　可是你不大容易动性子。
山 普 孙　我见了蒙太古家的狗子就生气。
葛莱古里　有胆量的，生了气就应当站住不动；逃跑的不是好汉。
山 普 孙　我见了他们家里的狗子，就会站住不动；蒙太古家的任何男女碰到了我，就像是碰到墙壁一样。
葛莱古里　这正说明你是个软弱无能的奴才；只有最没出息的家伙，才去墙底下躲难。
山 普 孙　的确不错；所以生来软弱的女人，就老是被人逼得不能动：我见了蒙太古家里人来，是男人，我就把他们从墙边推出去；是女人，我就把她们望着墙壁摔过去。
葛莱古里　吵架是咱们两家主仆男人们的事，与她们女人有什么相干？
山 普 孙　那我不管，我要做一个杀人不眨眼的魔王；一面跟男人们打架，一面对娘儿们也不留情面，我要她们的命。
葛莱古里　要娘儿们的性命吗？

SAMPSON	Ay, the heads of the maids, or their maidenheads. Take it in what sense thou wilt.
GREGORY	They must take it in sense that feel it.
SAMPSON	Me they shall feel while I am able to stand; and 'tis known I am a pretty piece of flesh.
GREGORY	'Tis well thou art not fish; if thou hadst, thou hadst been poor-John. Draw thy tool! Here comes two of the house of Montagues.

[*Enter two other Servingmen, Abram and Balthasar.*]

SAMPSON	My naked weapon is out. Quarrel! I will back thee.
GREGORY	How? turn thy back and run?
SAMPSON	Fear me not.
GREGORY	No, marry. I fear thee!
SAMPSON	Let us take the law of our sides; let them begin.
GREGORY	I will frown as I pass by, and let them take it as they list.
SAMPSON	Nay, as they dare. I will bite my thumb at them, which is disgrace to them if they bear it.
ABRAM	Do you bite your thumb at us, sir?
SAMPSON	I do bite my thumb, sir.
ABRAM	Do you bite your thumb at us, sir?
SAMPSON	[*Aside to Gregory.*] Is the law of our side if I say ay?
GREGORY	[*Aside to Sampson.*] No.
SAMPSON	No, sir, I do not bite my thumb at you, sir; but I bite my thumb, sir.
GREGORY	Do you quarrel, sir?
ABRAM	Quarrel, sir? No, sir.

山 普 孙	对了,娘儿们的性命,或是她们视同性命的童贞,你爱怎么说就怎么说。
葛莱古里	那就要看对方怎样感觉了。
山 普 孙	只要我下手,她们就会尝到我的辣手:就是有名的一身横肉呢。
葛莱古里	幸而你还不是一身鱼肉;否则你便是一条可怜虫了。拔出你的家伙来;有两个蒙太古家的人来啦。

（亚伯拉罕及鲍尔萨泽上）

山 普 孙	我的剑已经出鞘;你去跟他们吵起来,我就在你背后帮你的忙。
葛莱古里	怎么?你想转过背逃走吗?
山 普 孙	你放心吧,我不是那样的人。
葛莱古里	哼,我倒有点儿不放心!
山 普 孙	还是让他们先动手,打起官司来也是咱们的理直。
葛莱古里	我走过去向他们横个白眼,瞧他们怎么样。
山 普 孙	好,瞧他们有没有胆量。我要向他们咬我的大拇指,瞧他们能不能忍受这样的侮辱。
亚伯拉罕	你是向我们咬你的大拇指吗?
山 普 孙	我是咬我的大拇指。
亚伯拉罕	你是向我们咬你的大拇指吗?
山 普 孙	（向葛莱古里旁白）要是我说是,那么打起官司来是谁的理直?
葛莱古里	（向山普孙旁白）是他们的理直。
山 普 孙	不,我不是向你们咬我的大拇指;可是我是咬我的大拇指。
葛莱古里	你是要向我们挑衅吗?
亚伯拉罕	挑衅?不,哪儿的话。

SAMPSON	But if you do, sir, I am for you. I serve as good a man as you.
ABRAM	No better.
SAMPSON	Well, sir.
	[*Enter Benvolio.*]
GREGORY	[*aside to Sampson.*] Say 'better'. Here comes one of my master's kinsmen.
SAMPSON	Yes, better, sir.
ABRAM	You lie.
SAMPSON	Draw, if you be men. Gregory, remember thy swashing blow.
	[*They fight.*]
BENVOLIO	Part, fools! [*Beats down their swords.*]
	Put up your swords. you know not what you do.
	[*Enter Tybalt.*]
TYBALT	What, art thou drawn among these heartless hinds? Turn thee Benvolio! look upon thy death.
BENVOLIO	I do but keep the peace. Put up thy sword, Or manage it to part these men with me.
TYBALT	What, drawn, and talk of peace? I hate the word As I hate hell, all Montagues, and thee. Have at thee, coward!
	[*They fight.*]
	[*Enter an officer, and three four Citizens with clubs or partisans.*]
Officer	Clubs, bills, and partisans! Strike! beat them down!
Citizens	Down with the Capulets! Down with the Montagues!
	[*Enter Old Capulet in his gown, and his wife.*]
CAPULET	What noise is this? Give me my long sword, ho!

山普孙	你要是想跟我们吵架,那么我可以奉陪;你也是你家主子的奴才,我也是我家主子的奴才,难道我家的主子就比不上你家的主子?
亚伯拉罕	比不上。
山普孙	好。(班伏里奥上)
葛莱古里	(向山普孙旁白)说"比得上";我家老爷的一位亲戚来了。
山普孙	比得上。
亚伯拉罕	你胡说。
山普孙	是汉子就拔出剑来。葛莱古里,别忘了你的撒手锏。(双方互斗)
班伏里奥	分开,蠢材!(击下众仆的剑)收起你们的剑;你们不知道你们在干些什么事。

(提伯尔特上)

提伯尔特	怎么!你跟这些不中用的奴才吵架吗?过来,班伏里奥,让我结果你的性命。
班伏里奥	我不过维持和平;收起你的剑,或者帮我分开这些人。
提伯尔特	什么!你拔出了剑,还说什么和平?我痛恨这两个字,就跟我痛恨地狱、痛恨所有蒙太古家的人和你一样。照剑,懦夫!(二人相斗)

(两家各有若干人上,加入争斗;一群市民持枪棍继上)

众市民	打!打!打!把他们打下来!打倒凯普莱特!打倒蒙太古!

(凯普莱特穿长袍及凯普莱特夫人同上)

凯普莱特	什么事吵得这个样子?喂!把我的长剑拿来。

Wife	A crutch, a crutch! Why call you for a sword?
CAPULET	My sword, I say! Old Montague is come
	And flourishes his blade in spite of me.

[*Enter Old Montague and his wife.*]

MONTAGUE	Thou villain Capulet! — Hold me not, let me go.
Montague's Wife	Thou shalt not stir one foot to seek a foe.

[*Enter Prince Escalus, with his Train.*]

Prince	Rebellious subjects, enemies to peace,
	Profaners of this neighbour-stained steel —
	Will they not hear? What, ho! you men, you beasts,
	That quench the fire of your pernicious rage
	With purple fountains issuing from your veins!
	On pain of torture, from those bloody hands
	Throw your mistempered weapons to the ground
	And hear the sentence of your moved prince.
	Three civil brawls, bred of an airy word
	By thee, old Capulet, and Montague,
	Have thrice disturb'd the quiet of our streets
	And made Verona's ancient citizens
	Cast by their grave beseeming ornaments
	To wield old partisans, in hands as old,
	Cank'red with peace, to part your cank'red hate.
	If ever you disturb our streets again,
	Your lives shall pay the forfeit of the peace.
	For this time all the rest depart away.
	You, Capulet, shall go along with me;
	And, Montague, come you this afternoon,
	To know our farther pleasure in this case,
	To old Freetown, our common judgmentplace.

凯普莱特夫人 拐杖呢？拐杖呢？你要剑干什么？

凯 普 莱 特 快拿剑来！蒙太古那老东西来啦；他还晃着他的剑，明明在跟我寻事。

（蒙太古及蒙太古夫人上）

蒙 太 古 凯普莱特，你这奸贼！——别拉住我；让我走。

蒙 太 古 夫人你要去跟人家吵架，我连一步也不让你走。

（亲王率侍从上）

亲　　王 目无法纪的臣民，扰乱治安的罪人，你们的刀剑都被你们邻人的血玷污了；——他们不听我的话吗？喂，听着！你们这些人，你们这些畜生，你们为了扑灭你们怨毒的怒焰，不惜让殷红的流泉从你们的血管里喷涌出来；你们要是畏惧刑法，赶快把你们的凶器从你们血腥的手里丢下，静听你们震怒的君王的判决。凯普莱特，蒙太古，你们已经三次为了一句口头上的空言，引起了市民的械斗，扰乱了我们街道上的安宁，害得维罗纳的年老公民，也不能不脱下他们尊严的装束，在他们习于安乐的苍老衰弱的手里，掮过古旧的长枪，分解你们溃烂的纷争。要是你们以后再在市街上闹事，就要把你们的生命作为扰乱治安的代价。现在别人都给我退下去；凯普莱特，你跟我来；蒙太古，你今天下午到自由村的审判厅里来，听候我对于今天这一案

	Once more, on pain of death, all men depart.
	[*Exeunt all but Montague, his wife, and Benvolio.*]
MONTAGUE	Who set this ancient quarrel new abroach?
	Speak, nephew, were you by when it began?
BENVOLIO	Here were the servants of your adversary

And yours, close fighting ere I did approach.
I drew to part them. In the instant came
The fiery Tybalt, with his sword prepar'd;
Which, as he breath'd defiance to my ears,
He swung about his head and cut the winds,
Who, nothing hurt withal, hiss'd him in scorn.
While we were interchanging thrusts and blows,
Came more and more, and fought on part and part,
Till the Prince came, who parted either part.

Montague's Wife O, where is Romeo? Saw you him to-day?
Right glad I am he was not at this fray.

BENVOLIO Madam, an hour before the worshipp'd sun
Peer'd forth the golden window of the East,
A troubled mind drave me to walk abroad;
Where, underneath the grove of sycamore
That westward rooteth from this city's side,
So early walking did I see your son.
Towards him I made, but be was ware of me
And stole into the covert of the wood.
I— measuring his affections by my own,
Which then most sought where most might not be found,
Being one too many by my weary self,
Pursu'd my humour, not Pursuing his,

的宣判。大家散开去，倘有逗留不去的，格杀勿论！（除蒙太古夫妇及班伏里奥外皆下）

蒙　太　古　这一场宿怨是谁又重新煽风点火？侄儿，对我说，他们动手的时候，你也在场吗？

班伏里奥　我还没有到这儿来，您仇家的仆人跟您家里的仆人已经打成一团了。我拔出剑来分开他们；就在这时候，那个性如烈火的提伯尔特提着剑来了，他对我出言不逊，把剑在他自己头上舞得嗖嗖直响，就像风在那儿讥笑他的装腔作势一样。当我们正在剑来剑去的时候，人越来越多，有的帮这一面，有的帮那一面，乱哄哄地互相争斗，直等亲王来了，方才把两边的人喝开。

蒙太古夫人　啊，罗密欧呢？你今天见过他吗？我很高兴他没有参加这场争斗。

班伏里奥　伯母，在尊严的太阳开始从东方的黄金窗里探出头来的一小时以前，我因为心中烦闷，到郊外去散步，在城西一丛枫树的下面，我看见罗密欧兄弟一早在那儿走来走去。我正要向他走过去，他已经看见了我，就躲到树林深处去了。我因为自己也是心灰意懒，觉得连自己这一身也是多余的，只想找一处没有人迹的地方，所以凭着自己的心境推测别人的心境，也就不去

MONTAGUE	And gladly shunn'd who gladly fled from me. Many a morning hath he there been seen, With tears augmenting the fresh morning's dew, Adding to clouds more clouds with his deep sighs; But all so soon as the all-cheering sun Should in the farthest East begin to draw The shady curtains from Aurora's bed, Away from light steals home my heavy son And private in his chamber pens himself, Shuts up his windows, locks fair daylight out, And makes himself an artificial night. Black and portentous must this humour prove Unless good counsel may the cause remove.
BENVOLIO	My noble uncle, do you know the cause?
MONTAGUE	I neither know it nor can learn of him.
BENVOLIO	Have you importun'd him by any means?
MONTAGUE	Both by myself and many other friends; But he, his own affections' counsellor, Is to himself — I will not say how true — But to himself so secret and so close, So far from sounding and discovery, As is the bud bit with an envious worm Ere he can spread his sweet leaves to the air Or dedicate his beauty to the sun. Could we but learn from whence his sorrows grow, We would as willingly give cure as know. ［*Enter Romeo.*］
BENVOLIO	See, where he comes. So please you, step aside, I'll know his grievance, or be much denied.

找他多事，彼此互相避开了。

蒙　太　古　好多天的早上曾经有人在那边看见过他，用眼泪洒为清晨的露水，用长叹嘘成天空的云雾；可是一等到鼓舞众生的太阳在东方的天边开始揭起黎明女神床上灰黑色的帐幕的时候，我那怀着一颗沉重的心的儿子，就逃避了光明，溜回到家里；一个人关起了门躲在房间里，闭紧了窗子，把大好的阳光锁在外面，为他自己造成了一个人工的黑夜。他这一种怪脾气恐怕不是好兆，除非良言劝告可以替他解除心头的烦恼。

班伏里奥　伯父，您知道他的烦恼的根源吗？

蒙　太　古　我不知道，也没有法子从他自己嘴里探听出来。

班伏里奥　您有没有设法探问过他？

蒙　太　古　我自己以及许多其他的朋友都曾经探问过他，可是他把心事一古脑儿闷在自己肚里，总是守口如瓶，不让人家试探出来，正像一朵初生的蓓蕾，还没有迎风舒展它的嫩瓣，向太阳献吐它的娇艳，就给妒嫉的蛀虫咬啮了一样。只要能够知道他的悲哀究竟是从什么地方来的，我们一定会尽心竭力替他找寻治疗的方案。

（罗密欧上）

班伏里奥　瞧，他来了；请您站在一旁，等我去问问他究竟有些什么心事，看他理不理我。

MONTAGUE	I would thou wert so happy by thy stay
	To hear true shrift. Come, madam, let's away,
	[*Exeunt Montague and Wife.*]
BENVOLIO	Good morrow, cousin.
ROMEO	Is the day so young?
BENVOLIO	But new struck nine.
ROMEO	Ay me! sad hours seem long.
	Was that my father that went hence so fast?
BENVOLIO	It was. What sadness lengthens Romeo's hours?
ROMEO	Not having that which having makes them short.
BENVOLIO	In love?
ROMEO	Out —
BENVOLIO	Of love?
ROMEO	Out of her favour where I am in love.
BENVOLIO	Alas that Love, so gentle in his view,
	Should be so tyrannous and rough in proof!
ROMEO	Alas that Love, whose view is muffled still,
	Should without eyes see path ways to his will!
	Where shall we dine? O me! What fray was here?
	Yet tell me not, for I have heard it all.
	Here's much to do with hate, but more with love.
	Why then, O brawling love! O loving hate,
	O anything, of nothing first create!
	O heavy lightness, serious vanity!
	Misshapen chaos of well-seeming forms,
	Feather of lead, bright smoke, cold fire, sick health!
	Still-waking sleep, that is not what it is!
	This love feel I, that feel no love in this.
	Dost thou not laugh?

蒙太古	但愿你留在这儿,能够听到他的真情的吐露。来,夫人,我们去吧。(蒙太古夫妇同下)
班伏里奥	早安,兄弟。
罗密欧	天还是这样早吗?
班伏里奥	刚敲过九点钟。
罗密欧	唉!在悲哀里度过的时间似乎是格外长的。急急忙忙地走过去的那个人,不就是我的父亲吗?
班伏里奥	正是。什么悲哀使罗密欧的时间过得这样长?
罗密欧	因为我缺少了可以使时间变为短促的东西。
班伏里奥	你跌进恋爱的网里了吗?
罗密欧	我还在门外徘徊——
班伏里奥	在恋爱的门外?
罗密欧	我不能得到我的意中人的欢心。
班伏里奥	唉!想不到爱神的外表这样温柔,实际上却是如此残暴!
罗密欧	唉!想不到爱神蒙着眼睛,却会一直闯进人们的心灵!我们在什么地方吃饭?哎哟!又是谁在这儿打过架了?可是不必告诉我,我早就知道了。这些都是怨恨造成的后果,可是爱情的力量比它要大过许多。啊,吵吵闹闹的相爱,亲亲热热的怨恨!啊,无中生有的一切!啊,沉重的轻浮,严肃的狂妄,整齐的混乱,铅铸的羽毛,光明的烟雾,寒冷的火焰,憔悴的健康,永远觉醒的睡眠,否定的存在!我感觉到的爱情正是这么一种东西,可是我并不喜爱这一种爱情。你不会笑我吗?

BENVOLIO	No, coz, I rather weep.
ROMEO	Good heart, at what?
BENVOLIO	At thy good heart's oppression.
ROMEO	Why, such is love's transgression.
	Griefs of mine own lie heavy in my breast,
	Which thou wilt propagate, to have it prest
	With more of thine. This love that thou hast shown
	Doth add more grief to too much of mine own.
	Love is a smoke rais'd with the fume of sighs;
	Being purg'd, a fire sparkling in lovers' eyes;
	Being vex'd, a sea nourish'd with lovers' tears.
	What is it else? A madness most discreet,
	A choking gall, and a preserving sweet.
	Farewell, my coz. [*He turns to go.*]
BENVOLIO	Soft! I will go along.
	An if you leave me so, you do me wrong.
ROMEO	Tut! I have lost myself; I am not here;
	This is not Romeo, he's some other where.
BENVOLIO	Tell me in sadness, who is that you love?
ROMEO	What, shall I groan and tell thee?
BENVOLIO	Groan? Why no;
	But sadly tell me who.
ROMEO	Bid a sick man in sadness make his will.
	Ah, word ill urg'd to one that is so ill!
	In sadness, cousin, I do love a woman.
BENVOLIO	I aim'd so near when I suppos'd you lov'd.
ROMEO	A right good markman! And she's fair I love.
BENVOLIO	A right fair mark, fair coz, is soonest hit.
ROMEO	Well, in that hit you miss. She'll not be hit

班伏里奥 不,兄弟,我倒是有点儿想哭。

罗密欧 好人,为什么呢?

班伏里奥 因为瞧着你善良的心受到这样的痛苦。

罗密欧 唉!这就是爱情的错误,我自己已经有太多的忧愁重压在我的心头,你对我表示的同情,徒然使我在太多的忧愁之上再加上一重忧愁。爱情是叹息吹起的一阵烟;恋人的眼中有它净化了的火星;恋人的眼泪是它激起的波涛。此外呢?它又是最智慧的疯狂,哽喉的苦味,吃不到嘴的蜜糖。再见,兄弟。(欲去)

班伏里奥 且慢,让我跟你一块儿去;要是你就这样丢下了我,未免太不给我面子啦。

罗密欧 嘿!我已经遗失了我自己;我不在这儿;这不是罗密欧,他是在别的地方。

班伏里奥 老实告诉我,你所爱的是谁?

罗密欧 什么!你要我在痛苦呻吟中说出她的名字来吗?

班伏里奥 痛苦呻吟!不,你只要告诉我她是谁就得了。

罗密欧 叫一个病人郑重其事地立起遗嘱来!啊,对于一个病重的人,还有什么比这更刺痛他的心?老实对你说,兄弟,我是爱上了一个女人。

班伏里奥 我说你一定在恋爱,果然猜得不错。

罗密欧 好一个每发必中的射手!我所爱的是一位美貌的姑娘。

班伏里奥 好兄弟,目标越好,射得越准。

罗密欧 你这一箭就射岔了。丘比特的金箭不能射中她的心;

	With Cupid's arrow. She hath Dian's wit,
	And, in strong proof of chastity well arm'd,
	From Love's weak childish bow she lives unharm'd.
	She will not stay the siege of loving terms,
	Nor bide th' encounter of assailing eyes,
	Nor ope her lap to saint-seducing gold.
	O, she's rich in beauty; only poor
	That, when she dies, with beauty dies her store.
BENVOLIO	Then she hath sworn that she will still live chaste?
ROMEO	She hath, and in that sparing makes huge waste;
	For beauty, starv'd with her severity,
	Cuts beauty off from all posterity.
	She is too fair, too wise, wisely too fair,
	To merit bliss by making me despair.
	She hath forsworn to love, and in that vow
	Do I live dead that live to tell it now.
BENVOLIO	Be rul'd by me; forget to think of her.
ROMEO	O, teach me how I should forget to think!
BENVOLIO	By giving liberty unto thine eyes.
	Examine other beauties.
ROMEO	'Tis the way
	To call hers (exquisite) in question more.
	These happy masks that kiss fair ladies' brows,
	Being black puts us in mind they hide the fair.
	He that is strucken blind cannot forget
	The precious treasure of his eyesight lost.
	Show me a mistress that is passing fair,
	What doth her beauty serve but as a note
	Where I may read who pass'd that passing fair?

她有戴安娜女神的圣洁，不让爱情软弱的弓矢损害她的坚不可破的贞操。她不愿听任深怜蜜爱的词句把她包围，也不愿让灼灼逼人的眼光向她进攻，更不愿接受可以使圣人动心的黄金的诱惑。啊！美貌便是她巨大的财富，只可惜她一死以后，她的美貌也要化为黄土！

班伏里奥　那么她已经立誓终身守贞不嫁了吗？

罗密欧　她已经立下了这样的誓言，为了珍惜她自己，造成了莫大的浪费；因为她让美貌在无情的岁月中日渐枯萎，不知道替后世传留下她的绝世容华。她是个太美丽、太聪明的人儿，不应该剥夺她自身的幸福，使我抱恨终天。她已经立誓割舍爱情，我现在活着也就等于死去一般。

班伏里奥　听我的劝告，别再想起她了。

罗密欧　啊！那么你教我怎样忘记吧。

班伏里奥　你可以放纵你的眼睛，让它们多看几个世间的美人。

罗密欧　那不过格外使我觉得她的美艳无双罢了。那些吻着美人娇额的幸运的面罩，因为它们是黑色的缘故，常常使我们想起被它们遮掩的面庞不知多么娇丽。突然盲目的人，永远不会忘记存留在他消失了的视觉中的宝贵的影像。给我看一个姿容绝代的美人，她的美貌除

BENVOLIO	Farewell. Thou canst not teach me to forget.
	I'll pay that doctrine, or else die in debt.
	[*Exeunt.*]

SCENE II   The same. A street.

[*Enter Capulet, County Paris, and Servant — the Clown.*]

CAPULET	But Montague is bound as well as I,
	In penalty alike; and 'tis not hard, I think,
	For men so old as we to keep the peace.
PARIS	Of honourable reckoning are you both,
	And pity 'tis you liv'd at odds so long.
	But now, my lord, what say you to my suit?
CAPULET	But saying o'er what I have said before:
	My child is yet a stranger in the world,
	She hath not seen the change of fourteen years;
	Let two more summers wither in their pride
	Ere we may think his ripe to be a bride.
PARIS	Younger than she are happy mothers made.
CAPULET	And too soon marr'd are those so early made.
	The earth hath swallowed all my hopes but she;
	She is the hopeful lady of my earth.
	But woo her, gentle Paris, get her heart;
	My will to her consent is but a part.
	An she agree, within her scope of choice
	Lies my consent and fair according voice.
	This night I hold an old accustom'd feast,
	Whereto I have invited many a guest,

了使我记起世上有一个人比她更美以外,还有什么别的用处?再见,你不能教我怎样忘记。

班伏里奥 我一定要证明我的意见不错,否则死不瞑目。(同下)

第二场　同前。街道

(凯普莱特、帕里斯及仆人上)

凯普莱特 可是蒙太古也负着跟我同样的责任;我想像我们这样有了年纪的人,维持和平还不是难事。

帕里斯 你们两家都是很有名望的大族,结下了这样不解的冤仇,真是一件不幸的事。可是,老伯,您对于我的求婚有什么见教?

凯普莱特 我的意思早就对您表示过了。我的女儿今年还没有满十四岁,完全是一个不懂事的孩子;再过两个夏天,才可以谈到亲事。

帕里斯 比她年纪更小的人,都已经做了幸福的母亲了。

凯普莱特 早结果的树木一定早凋。我在这世上已经什么希望都没有了,只有她是我唯一的安慰。可是向她求爱吧,善良的帕里斯,得到她的欢心;只要她愿意,我的同意是没有问题的。今天晚上,我要按照旧例,举行一次宴会,邀请许多亲友参加;您也是我所要邀请的一

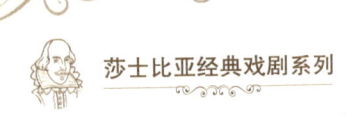

Such as I love; and you among the store,
One more, most welcome, makes my number more.
At my poor house look to behold this night
Earth-treading stars that make dark heaven light.
Such comfort as do lusty young men feel
When well apparell'd April on the heel
Of limping Winter treads, even such delight
Among fresh female buds shall you this night
Inherit at my house. Hear all, all see,
And like her most whose merit most shall be;
Which, on more view of many, mine, being one,
May stand in number, though in reck'ning none.
Come, go with me.

[*To Servant, giving him a paper.*]

Go, sirrah, trudge about
Through fair Verona; find those persons out
Whose names are written there, and to them say,
My house and welcome on their pleasure stay.

[*Exeunt Capulet and Paris.*]

Servant Find them out whose names are written here? It is written that the shoemaker should meddle with his yard and the tailor with his last, the fisher with his pencil and the painter with his nets; but I am sent to find those persons whose names are here writ, and can never find what names the writing person hath here writ. I must to the learned. In good time!

[*Enter Benvolio and Romeo.*]

BENVOLIO Tut, man, one fire burns out another's burning;
One pain is lessoned by another's anguish;

个,请您接受我最诚意的欢迎。在我的寒舍里,今晚您可以见到灿烂的群星翩然下降,照亮黑暗的天空;在蓓蕾一样娇艳的女郎丛里,您可以充分享受青春的愉快,正像盛装的四月追随着残冬的足迹降临人世,在年轻人的心里充满着活跃的欢欣一样。您可以听个够,看个饱,从许多美貌的女郎中间,连我的女儿也在内,拣一个最好的做您的意中人。来,跟我去。(以一纸交仆)你到维罗纳全城去走一转,挨着这单子上一个一个的名字去找人,请他们到我的家里来。(凯普莱特、帕里斯同下)

仆　　人　挨着这单子上的名字去找人!人家说,鞋匠的针线,裁缝的钉锤,渔夫的笔,画师的网,各人有各人的职司;可是我们的老爷却叫我挨着这单子上的名字去找人,我怎么知道写字的人在这上面写着些什么?我一定要找个识字的人。来得正好。

(班伏里奥及罗密欧上)

班伏里奥　不,兄弟,新的火焰可以把旧的火焰扑灭,大的苦痛可以使小的苦痛减轻;头晕目眩的时候,只要转身向后;一桩绝望的忧伤,也可以用另一桩烦恼把它驱除。

	Turn giddy, and be holp by backward turning;
	One desperate grief cures with another's languish.
	Take thou some new infection to thy eye,
	And the rank poison of the old will die.
ROMEO	Your plantain leaf is excellent for that.
BENVOLIO	For what, I pray thee?
ROMEO	For your broken shin.
BENVOLIO	Why, Romeo, art thou mad?
ROMEO	Not mad, but bound more than a madman is;
	Shut up in Prison, kept without my food,
	Whipp'd and tormented and—God-den, good fellow.
Servant	God gi' go-den. I pray, sir, can you read?
ROMEO	Ay, mine own fortune in my misery.
Servant	Perhaps you have learned it without book. But, I pray, can you read anything you see?
ROMEO	Ay, If I know the letters and the language.
Servant	Ye say honestly. Rest you merry! [*He turns to go.*]
ROMEO	Stay, fellow; I can read.

[*He reads.*]

'Signior Martino and his wife and daughters;

County Anselmo and his beauteous sisters;

The lady widow of Vitruvio;

Signior Placentio and His lovely nieces;

Mercutio and his brother Valentine;

Mine uncle Capulet, his wife, and daughters;

My fair niece Rosaline and Livia;

Signior Valentio and His cousin Tybalt;

Lucio and the lively Helena. '

[*Gives back the paper.*]

给你的眼睛找一个新的迷惑，你原来的痼疾就可以霍然脱体。

罗　密　欧　你的药草只好医治——
班伏里奥　医治什么？请问。
罗　密　欧　医治你的跌伤的胫骨。
班伏里奥　怎么，罗密欧，你疯了吗？
罗　密　欧　我没有疯，可是比疯人更不自由；关在牢狱里，不进饮食，挨受着鞭挞和酷刑——晚安，好朋友！
仆　　　人　晚安！请问先生，您念过书吗？
罗　密　欧　是的，这是我的不幸中的资产。
仆　　　人　也许您只会背诵，可是请问您会不会看着字一个一个地念？
罗　密　欧　我认得的字，我就会念。
仆　　　人　您说得很老实；上帝保佑您！（欲去）
罗　密　欧　等一等，朋友；我会念。（罗密欧念道）"玛丁诺先生暨夫人及诸位令爱，安赛尔美伯爵及诸位令妹；寡居之维特鲁维奥夫人；帕拉森西奥先生及诸位令侄女；茂丘西奥及其令弟凡伦丁；凯普莱特叔父暨婶母及诸位贤妹；罗瑟琳贤侄女；里维娅；伐伦西奥先生及其令表弟提伯尔特；路西奥及活泼之海丽娜。"（交还

	A fair assembly. Whither should they come?
Servant	Up.
ROMEO	Whither? To supper?
Servant	To our house.
ROMEO	Whose house?
Servant	My master's.
ROMEO	Indeed I should have ask'd you that before.
Servant	Now I'll tell you without asking. My master is the great rich Capulet; and if you be not of the house of Montagues, I pray come and crush a cup of wine. Rest you merry!

[*Exit.*]

BENVOLIO At this same ancient feast of Capulet's
Sups the fair Rosaline whom thou so lov'st;
With all the admired beauties of Verona.
Go thither, and with unattainted eye
Compare her face with some that I shall show,
And I will make thee think thy swan a crow.

ROMEO When the devout religion of mine eye
Maintains such falsehood, then turn tears to fires;
And these, who, often drown'd, could never die,
Transparent heretics, be burnt for liars!
One fairer than my love? The all-seeing sun
Ne'er saw her match since first the world begun.

BENVOLIO Tut! you saw her fair, none else being by,
Herself pois'd with herself in either eye;
But in that crystal scales let there be weigh'd
Your lady's love against some other maid
That I will show you shining at this feast,

罗密欧与朱丽叶
ROMEO AND JULIET

此纸）好一群名士贤媛！请他们到什么地方去？

仆　　　　人　到——

罗　密　欧　哪里？

仆　　　　人　到我们家里吃饭去。

罗　密　欧　谁的家里？

仆　　　　人　我的主人的家里。

罗　密　欧　对了，我该先问你的主人是谁才是。

仆　　　　人　您也不用问了，我就告诉您吧。我的主人就是那个有财有势的凯普莱特；要是您不是蒙太古家里的人，请您也来跟我们喝一杯酒，愿您一生快乐！（下）

班伏里奥　在这一个凯普莱特家里按照旧例举行的宴会中间，你所热恋的美人罗瑟琳也要跟着维罗纳城里所有的绝色名媛一同去赴宴。你也到那儿去吧，用着不带成见的眼光，把她的容貌跟别人比较比较，你就可以知道你的天鹅不过是一只乌鸦罢了。

罗　密　欧　要是我的虔敬的眼睛会相信这种谬误的幻象，那么让眼泪变成火焰，把这一双罪状昭著的异教邪徒烧成灰烬吧！比我的爱人还美！烛照万物的太阳，自有天地以来也不曾看见过一个可以和她媲美的人。

班伏里奥　嘿！你看见她的时候，因为没有别人在旁边，你的两只眼睛里只有她一个人，所以你以为她是美丽的；可是在你那水晶的天秤里，要是把你的恋人跟另外一个我可以在这宴会里指点给你看的美貌的姑娘同时较量

	And she shall scant show well that now seems best.
ROMEO	I'll go along, no such sight to be shown,
	But to rejoice in splendour of my own.
	[*Exeunt.*]

SCENE III   The same. Capulet's house.

[*Enter Capulet's wife, and Nurse.*]

Wife	Nurse, where's my daughter? Call her forth to me.
Nurse	Now, by my maidenhead at twelve year old,
	I bade her come. What, lamb! what ladybird!
	God fobid! Where's this girl? What, Juliet!

[*Enter Juliet.*]

JULIET	How now? who calls?
Nurse	Your mother.
JULIET	Madam, I am here.
	What is your will?
Wife	This is the matter. — Nurse, give leave awhile,
	We must talk in secret. Nurse, come back again;
	I have rememb'red me, thou's hear our counsel.
	Thou knowest my daughter's of a pretty age.
Nurse	Faith, I can tell her age unto an hour.
Wife	She's not fourteen.
Nurse	I'll lay fourteen of my teeth —
	And yet, to my teen be it spoken, I have but four —
	She is not fourteen. How long is it now To Lammas-tide?
Wife	A fortnight and odd days.
Nurse	Even or odd, of all days in the year,

起来，那么她现在虽然仪态万方，那时候就要自惭形秽了。

罗密欧　我倒要去这一次；不是去看你所说的美人，只要看看我自己的爱人怎样大放光彩，我就心满意足了。（同下）

第三场　同前。凯普莱特家中一室

（凯普莱特夫人及乳母上）

凯普莱特夫人　奶妈，我的女儿呢？叫她出来见我。

乳　母　凭着我十二岁时候的童贞发誓，我早就叫过她了。喂，小绵羊！喂，小鸟儿！上帝保佑！这孩子到什么地方去啦？喂，朱丽叶！

（朱丽叶上）

朱丽叶　什么事？谁叫我？

乳　母　你的母亲。

朱丽叶　母亲，我来了。您有什么吩咐？

凯普莱特夫人　是这么一件事。奶妈，你出去一会儿。我们要谈些秘密的话。——奶妈，你回来吧；我想起来了，你也应当听听我们的谈话。你知道我的女儿年纪也不算怎么小啦。

乳　母　对啊，我把她的生辰记得清清楚楚的。

凯普莱特夫人　她现在还不满十四岁。

乳　母　我可以用我的十四颗牙齿打赌——唉，说来伤心，我的牙齿掉得只剩四颗啦！——她还没有满十四岁呢。现在离收获节还有多久？

凯普莱特夫人　两个星期多一点。

乳　母　不多不少，不先不后，到收获节的晚上她才满十四岁。

Come Lammas Eve at night shall she be fourteen.
Susan and she (God rest all Christian souls!)
Were of an age. Well, Susan is with God;
She was too good for me. But, as I said,
On Lammas Eve at night shall she be fourteen;
That shall she, marry; I remember it well.
'Tis since the earthquake now eleven years;
And she was wean'd (I never shall forget it),
Of all the days of the year, upon that day:
For I had then laid wormwood to my dug,
Sitting in the sun under the dovehouse wall.
My lord and you were then at Mantua.
Nay, I do bear a brain. But, as I said,
When it did taste the wormwood on the nipple
Of my dug and felt it bitter, pretty fool,
To see it tetchy and fall out with the dug!
Shake, quoth the dovehouse! 'Twas no need, I trow,
To bid me trudge.
And since that time it is eleven years,
For then she could stand high-lone; nay, by th' rood,
She could have run and waddled all about;
For even the day before, she broke her brow;
And then my husband (God be with his soul!
'A was a merry man) took up the child.
'Yea,' quoth he, 'dost thou fall upon thy face?
Thou wilt fall backward when thou hast more wit;
Wilt thou not, Jule?' and, by my holidam,
The pretty wretch left crying, and said 'Ay.'
To see now how a jest shall come about!

苏珊跟她同年——上帝安息一切基督徒的灵魂！唉！苏珊是跟上帝在一起啦，我命里不该有这样一个孩子。可是我说过的，到收获节的晚上，她就要满十四岁啦；正是，一点不错，我记得清清楚楚的。自从地震那一年到现在，已经十一年啦；那时候她已经断了奶，我永远不会忘记，不先不后，刚巧在那一天；因为我在那时候用艾叶涂在奶头上，坐在鸽棚下面晒着太阳；老爷跟您那时候都在曼图亚。瞧，我的记性可不算坏。可是我说的，她一尝到我奶头上的艾叶的味道，觉得变苦啦，哎哟，这可爱的小傻瓜！她就发起脾气来，把奶头甩开啦。那时候地震，鸽棚都在摇动呢。这个说来话长，算来也有十一年啦；后来她就慢慢地会一个人站得直挺挺的，还会摇呀摆的到处乱跑，就是在她跌破额角的那一天，我那去世的丈夫——上帝安息他的灵魂！他是个喜欢说说笑笑的人，把这孩子抱了起来，"啊！"他说，"你往前扑了吗？等你年纪一大，你就要往后仰了；是不是呀，朱丽？"谁知道这个可爱的坏东西忽然停住了哭声，说"嗯。"哎哟，真把

	I warrant, an I should live a thousand years,
	I never should forget it. 'Wilt thou not, Jule?' quoth he,
	And, pretty fool, it stinted, and said 'Ay.'
Wife	Enough of this. I pray thee hold thy peace.
Nurse	Yes, madam. Yet I cannot choose but laugh
	To think it should leave crying and say 'Ay.'
	And yet, I warrant, it had upon it brow
	A bump as big as a young cock'rel's stone;
	A perilous knock; and it cried bitterly.
	'Yea,' quoth my husband, 'fall'st upon thy face?
	Thou wilt fall backward when thou comest to age;
	Wilt thou not, Julie?' It stinted, and said 'Ay.'
JULIET	And stint thou too, I pray thee, nurse, say I.
Nurse	Peace, I have done. God mark thee to his grace!
	Thou wast the prettiest babe that e'er I nurs'd.
	An I might live to see thee married once,
	I have my wish.
Wife	Marry, that 'marry' is the very theme
	I came to talk of. Tell me, daughter Juliet,
	How stands your disposition to be married?
JULIET	It is an honour that I dream not of.
Nurse	An honour? Were not I thine only nurse,
	I would say thou hadst suck'd wisdom from thy teat.
Wife	Well, think of marriage now. Younger than you,
	Here in Verona, ladies of esteem,
	Are made already mothers. By my count,
	I was your mother much upon these years
	That you are now a maid. Thus then in brief:
	The valiant Paris seeks you for his love.

人都笑死了!要是我活到一千岁,我也再不会忘记这句话。"是不是呀,朱丽?"他说;这可爱的小傻瓜就停住了哭声,说"嗯。"

凯普莱特夫人 得了得了,请你别说下去了吧。

乳　　母 是,太太。可是我一想到她会停住了哭说"嗯",就禁不住笑起来。不说假话,她额角上肿起了像小雄鸡的睾丸那么大的一个包哩;她痛得放声大哭;"啊!"我的丈夫说,"你往前扑了吗?等你年纪一大,你就要往后仰了;是不是呀,朱丽?"她就停住了哭声,说"嗯。"

朱　丽　叶 我说,奶妈,你也可以停住嘴了。

乳　　母 好,我不说啦,我不说啦。上帝保佑你!你是在我手里抚养长大的一个最可爱的小宝贝;要是我能够活到有一天瞧着你嫁了出去,也算了结我的一桩心愿啦。

凯普莱特夫人 是呀,我现在就是要谈起她的亲事。朱丽叶,我的孩子,告诉我,要是现在把你嫁了出去,你觉得怎么样?

朱　丽　叶 这是我做梦也没有想到过的一件荣誉。

乳　　母 一件荣誉!倘不是你只有我这一个奶妈,我一定要说你的聪明是从奶头上得来的。

凯普莱特夫人 好,现在你把婚姻问题考虑考虑吧。在这维罗纳城里,比你再年轻点儿的千金小姐们,都已经做了母亲啦。就拿我来说吧,我在你现在这样的年纪,也已经生下了你。废话用不着多说,少年英俊的帕里斯已经来向你求过婚啦。

Nurse	A man, young lady! lady, such a man
	As all the world — Why he's a man of wax.
Wife	Verona's summer hath not such a flower.
Nurse	Nay, he's a flower, in faith— a very flower.
Wife	What say you? Can you love the gentleman?
	This night you shall behold him at our feast.
	Read o'er the volume of young Paris' face,
	And find delight writ there with beauty's pen;
	Examine every married lineament,
	And see how one another lends content;
	And what obscur'd in this fair volume lies
	Find written in the margent of his eyes.
	This precious book of love, this unbound lover,
	To beautify him only lacks a cover.
	The fish lives in the sea, and 'tis much pride
	For fair without the fair within to hide.
	That book in many's eyes doth share the glory,
	That in gold clasps locks in the golden story;
	So shall you share all that he doth possess,
	By having him making yourself no less.
Nurse	No less? Nay, bigger! Women grow by men.
Wife	Speak briefly, can you like of Paris' love?
JULIET	I'll look to like, if looking liking move;
	But no more deep will I endart mine eye
	Than your consent gives strength to make it fly.
	[Enter Servingman.]
Servant	Madam, the guests are come, supper serv'd up, you call'd, my young lady ask'd for, the nurse curs'd in the pantry, and everything in extremity. I must hence to

乳　　　母	真是一位好官人，小姐！像这样的一个男人，小姐，真是天下少有。哎哟！他真是一位十全十美的好郎君。
凯普莱特夫人	维罗纳的夏天找不到这样一朵好花。
乳　　　母	是啊，他是一朵花，真是一朵好花。
凯普莱特夫人	你怎么说？你能不能喜欢这个绅士？今晚上在我们家里的宴会中间，你就可以看见他。从年轻的帕里斯的脸上，你可以读到用秀美的笔写成的迷人诗句；一根根齐整的线条，交织成整个一幅谐和的图画；要是你想探索这一卷美好的书中的奥秘，在他的眼角上可以找到微妙的诠释。这本珍贵的恋爱的经典，只缺少一帧可以使它相得益彰的封面；正像游鱼需要活水，美妙的内容也少不了美妙的外表陪衬。记载着金科玉律的宝籍，锁合在漆金的封面里，它的辉煌富丽为众目所共见；要是你做了他的封面，那么他所有的一切都属于你所有了。
乳　　　母	何止如此！我们女人有了男人就富足了。
凯普莱特夫人	简简单单地回答我，你能够接受帕里斯的爱吗？
朱　丽　叶	要是我看见了他以后，能够发生好感，那么我是准备喜欢他的。可是我的眼光是飞箭，倘然没有得到您的允许，是不敢大胆发射出去的呢。

（一仆人上）

| 仆　　　人 | 太太，客人都来了，餐席已经摆好了，请您跟小姐快些出去。大家在厨房里埋怨着奶妈，什么都乱成一团。 |

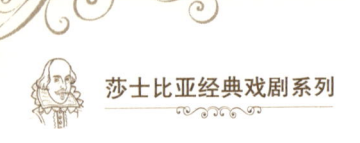

	wait. I beseech you follow straight.
Wife	We follow thee. [*Exit Servingman.*]
	Juliet, the County stays.
Nurse	Go, girl, seek happy nights to happy days.
	[*Exeunt.*]

SCENE IV   The same. A street.

[*Enter Romeo, Mercutio, Benvolio, with five or six other Maskers; Torchbearers.*]

ROMEO   What, shall this speech be spoke for our excuse?
Or shall we on without apology?

BENVOLIO   The date is out of such prolixity.
We'll have no Cupid hoodwink'd with a scarf,
Bearing a Tartar's painted bow of lath,
Scaring the ladies like a crow keeper;
[Nor no without-book prologue, faintly spoke
After the prompter, for our entrance;]
But, let them measure us by what they will,
We'll measure them a measure, and be gone.

ROMEO   Give me a torch. I am not for this ambling.
Being but heavy, I will bear the light.

MERCUTIO   Nay, gentle Romeo, we must have you dance.

ROMEO   Not I, believe me. You have dancing shoes
With nimble soles; I have a soul of lead
So stakes me to the ground I cannot move.

MERCUTIO   You are a lover. Borrow Cupid's wings
And soar with them above a common bound

ROMEO   I am too sore enpierced with his shaft

　　　　　　　我要侍候客人去；请您马上就来。（仆人下）
凯普莱特夫人　我们就来了。朱丽叶，那伯爵在等着呢。
乳　　　母　去，孩子，快去找天天欢乐，夜夜良宵。（同下）

第四场　同前。街道

（罗密欧、茂丘西奥、班伏里奥及五六人或戴假面或持火炬上）

罗　密　欧　怎么！我们就用这一番话作为我们的进身之阶呢，还是就这么昂然直入，不说一句道歉的话？

班伏里奥　这种虚文俗套，现在早就不流行了。我们用不着蒙着眼睛的丘比特，背着一张花漆的木弓，像个稻草人似的去吓那些娘儿们；也用不着跟着提示的人一句一句念那从书上默诵出来的登场白；随他们把我们认作什么人，我们只要跳完一回舞，走了就完啦。

罗　密　欧　给我一个火炬，我不高兴跳舞。我的阴沉的心需要着光明。

茂丘西奥　不，好罗密欧，我们一定要你陪着我们跳舞。

罗　密　欧　我实在不能跳。你们都有轻快的舞鞋；我只有一个铅一样重的灵魂，把我的身体紧紧地钉在地上，使我的脚步不能移动。

茂丘西奥　你是一个恋人，你就借着丘比特的翅膀，高高地飞起来吧。

罗　密　欧　他的羽镞已经穿透我的胸膛，我不能借着他的羽翼高

	To soar with his light feathers; and so bound
	I cannot bound a pitch above dull woe.
	Under love's heavy burthen do I sink.
MERCUTIO	And, to sink in it, should you burthen love—
	Too great oppression for a tender thing.
ROMEO	Is love a tender thing? It is too rough,
	Too rude, too boist'rous, and it pricks like thorn.
MERCUTIO	If love be rough with you, be rough with love.
	Prick love for pricking, and you beat love down.
	Give me a case to put my visage in. [*Putting on a mask.*]
	A visor for a visor! What care I
	What curious eye doth quote deformities?
	Here are the beetle brows shall blush for me.
BENVOLIO	Come, knock and enter; and no sooner in
	But every man betake him to his legs.
ROMEO	A torch for me! Let wantons light of heart
	Tickle the senseless rushes with their heels;
	For I am proverb'd with a grandsire phrase,
	I'll be a candle-holder and look on;
	The game was ne'er so fair, and I am done.
MERCUTIO	Tut! dun's the mouse, the constable's own word!
	If thou art Dun, we'll draw thee from the mire
	Of this sir-reverence love, wherein thou stick'st
	Up to the ears. Come, we burn daylight, ho!
ROMEO	Nay, that's not so.
MERCUTIO	I mean, sir, in delay
	We waste our lights in vain, like lamps by day.
	Take our good meaning, for our judgment sits

翔；他束缚住了我整个的灵魂，爱的重担压得我向下坠沉，跳不出烦恼去。

茂丘西奥 爱是一件温柔的东西，要是你拖着它一起沉下去，那未免太难为它了。

罗 密 欧 爱是温柔的吗？它是太粗暴、太专横、太野蛮了；它像荆棘一样刺人。

茂丘西奥 要是爱情虐待了你，你也可以虐待爱情；它刺痛了你，你也可以刺痛它；这样你就可以战胜了爱情。给我一个面具，让我把我的尊容藏起来；（戴假面）哎哟，好难看的鬼脸！再给我拿一个面具来把它罩住吧。也罢，就让人家笑我丑，也有这一张鬼脸替我遮羞。

班伏里奥 来，敲门进去；大家一进门，就跳起舞来。

罗 密 欧 拿一个火炬给我。让那些无忧无虑的公子哥儿们去卖弄他们的舞步吧；莫怪我说句老气横秋的话，我对于这种玩意儿实在敬谢不敏，还是做个壁上旁观的人吧。

茂丘西奥 胡说！要是你已经没头没脑深陷在恋爱的泥沼里——恕我说这样的话——那么我们一定要拉你出来。来来来，我们别白昼点灯浪费光阴啦！

罗 密 欧 我们并没有白昼点灯。

茂丘西奥 我的意思是说，我们耽误时光，好比白昼点灯一样。我们没有恶意，我们还有五个官能，可以有五倍的观

	Five times in that ere once in our five wits.
ROMEO	And we mean well, in going to this masque;
	But 'tis no wit to go.
MERCUTIO	Why, may one ask?
ROMEO	I dreamt a dream to-night.
MERCUTIO	And so did I.
ROMEO	Well, what was yours?
MERCUTIO	That dreamers often lie.
ROMEO	In bed asleep, while they do dream things true.
MERCUTIO	O, then I see Queen Mab hath been with you.
BENVOLIO	Queen Mab! What's she!
MERCUTIO	She is the fairies' midwife, and she comes
	In shape no bigger than an agate stone
	On the forefinger of an alderman,
	Drawn with a team of little atomies
	Athwart men's noses as they lie asleep;
	Her wagon spokes made of long spinners' legs,
	The cover, of the winges of grasshoppers;
	Her traces, of the smallest spider's web;
	Her collars, of the moonshine's wat'ry beams;
	Her whip, of cricket's bone; the lash, of film;
	Her wagoner, a small grey-coated gnat,
	Not half so big as a round little worm
	Prick'd from the lazy finger of a maid;
	Her chariot is an empty hazelnut,
	Made by the joiner squirrel or old grub,
	Time out o' mind the fairies' coachmakers.
	And in this state she gallops night by night
	Through lovers' brains, and then they dream of love;

察能力呢。

罗 密 欧　我们去参加他们的舞会也无恶意,只怕不是一件聪明的事。

茂丘西奥　为什么?请问。

罗 密 欧　昨天晚上我做了一个梦。

茂丘西奥　我也做了一个梦。

罗 密 欧　好,你做了什么梦?

茂丘西奥　我梦见做梦的人老是说谎。

罗 密 欧　一个人在睡梦里往往可以见到真实的事情。

茂丘西奥　啊!那么一定春梦婆来望过你了。

班伏里奥　春梦婆!她是谁?

茂丘西奥　她是精灵们的稳婆;她的身体只有郡吏手指上一颗玛瑙那么大;几匹蚂蚁大小的细马替她拖着车子,越过酣睡的人们的鼻梁,她的车辐是用蜘蛛的长脚做成的;车篷是蚱蜢的翅膀;挽索是小蜘蛛丝,颈带是如水的月光;马鞭是蟋蟀的骨头;缰绳是天际的游丝。替她驾车的是一只小小的灰色的蚊虫,它的大小还不及从一个贪懒丫头的指尖上挑出来的懒虫的一半。她的车子是野蚕用一个榛子的空壳替她造成,它们从古以来就是精灵们的车匠。她每夜驱着这样的车子,穿过情人们的脑中,他们就会在梦里谈情说爱;经过官员们

O'er courtiers' knees, that dream on curtsies straight;
O'er lawyers' fingers, who straight dream on fees;
O'er ladies' lips, who straight on kisses dream,
Which oft the angry Mab with blisters plagues,
Because their breaths with sweetmeats tainted are.
Sometime she gallops o'er a courtier's nose,
And then dreams he of smelling out a suit;
And sometime comes she with a tithe-pig's tail
Tickling a parson's nose as 'a lies asleep,
Then dreams he of another benefice.
Sometimes she driveth o'er a soldier's neck,
And then dreams he of cutting foreign throats,
Of breaches, ambuscadoes, Spanish blades,
Of healths five fadom deep; and then anon
Drums in his ear, at which he starts and wakes,
And being thus frighted, swears a prayer or two
And sleeps again. This is that very Mab
That plats the manes of horses in the night
And bakes the eftlocks in foul sluttish hairs,
Which once untangled much misfortune bodes
This is the hag, when maids lie on their backs,
That presses them and learns them first to bear,
Making them women of good carriage.
This is she —

ROMEO   Peace, peace, Mercutio, peace!
Thou talk'st of nothing.

MERCUTIO   True, I talk of dreams;
Which are the children of an idle brain,
Begot of nothing but vain fantasy;

的膝上，他们就会在梦里打躬作揖；经过律师们的手指，他们就会在梦里伸手讨讼费；经过娘儿们的嘴唇，她们就会在梦里跟人家接吻，可是因为春梦婆讨厌她们嘴里吐出来的糖果的气息，往往罚她们满嘴长着水泡。有时奔驰过廷臣的鼻子，他就会在梦里寻找好差事；有时她从捐献给教会的猪身上拔下它的尾巴来，撩拨着一个牧师的鼻孔，他就会梦见自己又领到一份俸禄；有时她绕过一个兵士的颈项，他就会梦见杀敌人的头，进攻、埋伏、锐利的剑锋、淋漓的痛饮——忽然被耳边的鼓声惊醒，咒骂了几句，又翻了个身睡去了。就是这一个春梦婆在夜里把马鬣打成了辫子，把懒女人的龌龊的乱发烘成一处处胶粘的硬块，倘然把它们梳通了，就要遭逢祸事；就是这个婆子在人家女孩子们仰面睡觉的时候，压在她们的身上，教会她们怎样养儿子；就是她——

罗密欧　得啦，得啦，茂丘西奥，别说啦！你全然在那儿痴人说梦。

茂丘西奥　对了，梦本来是痴人脑中的胡思乱想；它的本质像空气一样稀薄；它的变化莫测，就像一阵风，刚才还在

	Which is as thin of substance as the air,
	And more inconstant than the wind, who wooes
	Even now the frozen bosom of the North
	And, being anger'd, puffs away from thence,
	Turning his side to the dew-dropping South.
BENVOLIO	This wind you talk of blows us from ourselves.
	Supper is done, and we shall come too late.
ROMEO	I fear, too early; for my mind misgives
	Some consequence, yet hanging in the stars,
	Shall bitterly begin his fearful date
	With this night's revels and expire the term
	Of a despised life, clos'd in my breast,
	By some vile forfeit of untimely death.
	But he that hath the steerage of my course
	Direct my sail! On, lusty gentlemen!
BENVOLIO	Strike, drum.
	[Exeunt.]

SCENE V   The same. Capulet's house.

[They march about the stage, and Servingmen come forth with napkins.]

First Servant Where's Potpan, that he helps not to take away? He shift a trencher! he scrape a trencher!

Second Servant When good manners shall lie all in one or two men's hands, and they unwash'd too, 'tis a foul thing.

First Servant Away with the join-stools, remove the court-cubbert, look to the plate. Good thou, save me a piece of marchpane and, as thou loves me, let the porter let in

向着冰雪的北方求爱,忽然发起恼来,一转身又到雨露的南方来了。

班伏里奥　你讲起的这一阵风,不知把我们自己吹到哪儿去了。人家晚饭都用过了,我们进去怕要太晚啦。

罗　密　欧　我怕也许是太早了;我仿佛觉得有一种不可知的命运,将要从我们今天晚上的狂欢开始它的恐怖的统治,我这可憎恨的生命,将要遭遇残酷的夭折而告一结束。可是让支配我的前途的上帝指导我的行动吧!前进,快活的朋友们!

班伏里奥　来,把鼓擂起来。(同下)

第五场　同前。凯普莱特家中厅堂

(乐工各持乐器等候;众仆上)

仆　甲　卜得潘呢?他怎么不来帮忙把这些盘子拿下去?他不愿意搬碟子!他不愿意揩砧板!

仆　乙　一切事情都交给一两个人管,叫他们连洗手的工夫都没有,这真糟糕!

仆　甲　把折凳拿进去,把食器架搬开,留心打碎盘子。好兄弟,留一块杏仁酥给我;谢谢你去叫那管门的让苏珊跟耐

Susan Grindstone and Nell.

[*Exit second servingmen.*] Antony, and Potpan!

[*Enter two more servingmen.*]

Second Servant Ay, boy, ready.

First Servant You are look'd for and call'd for, ask'd for and sought for, in the great chamber.

Third Servant We cannot be here and there too. Cheerly, boy! Be brisk awhile, and the longer liver take all.

[*Exeunt third and fourth seningmen.*]

[*Enter Capulet, his wife, Juliet, Tybalt, Nurse and all the Guests and Gentlewomen to the Maskers.*]

CAPULET Welcome, gentlemen! Ladies that have their toes
Unplagu'd with corns will have a bout with you.
Ah ha, my mistresses! which of you all
Will now deny to dance? She that makes dainty,
She I'll swear hath corns. Am I come near ye now?
Welcome, gentlemen! I have seen the day
That I have worn a visor and could tell
A whispering tale in a fair lady's ear,
Such as would please. 'Tis gone, 'tis gone, 'tis gone!
You are welcome, gentlemen! Come, musicians, play.

[*Music plays, and they dance.*]

A hall, a hall! give room! and foot it, girls.
More light, you knaves! and turn the tables up,
And quench the fire, the room is grown too hot.
Ah, sirrah, this unlook'd-for sport comes well.
Nay, sit, nay, sit, good cousin Capulet,
For you and I are past our dancing days.
How long is't now since last yourself and I

儿进来。（仆乙下）安东尼！卜得潘！

（另两仆上）

仆　　乙　噢，兄弟，我在这儿。

仆　　甲　里头在找着你，叫着你，问着你，到处寻着你。

仆　　丙　我们可不能一身分两处呀。来，孩子们，大家出力！（众仆退后）

（凯普莱特夫妇、朱丽叶、提伯尔特、乳母自一方上；众宾客及假面跳舞者等自另一方上，相遇）

凯普莱特　诸位朋友，欢迎欢迎！足趾上不生茧子的小姐太太们要跟你们跳一回舞呢。啊哈！我的小姐们，你们中间现在有什么人不愿意跳舞？我可以发誓，谁要是推三阻四的，一定脚上长着老大的茧子；果然给我猜中了吗？诸位朋友，欢迎欢迎！我从前也曾经戴过假面，在一个标致姑娘的耳朵旁边讲些使得她心花怒放的话儿；这种时代现在是过去了，过去了，过去了。诸位朋友，欢迎欢迎！来，乐工们，奏起音乐来吧。（奏乐；众人开始跳舞）站开些！站开些！让出地方来。姑娘们，跳起来吧。混蛋，把灯点亮一点，把桌子一起搬掉，把火炉熄了，这屋子里太热啦。啊，好小子！这才玩得高兴。啊！

	Were in a mask?
Second Capulet	By'r lady, thirty years.
CAPULET	What, man! 'Tis not so much, 'tis not so much!
	'Tis since the nuptial of Lucentio,
	Come Pentecost as quickly as it will,
	Some five-and-twenty years, and then we mask'd.
Second Capulet	'Tis more, 'tis more. His son is elder, sir;
	His son is thirty.
CAPULET	Will you tell me that?
	His son was but a ward two years ago.
ROMEO	[*To a Servingman.*] What lady's that, which doth enrich the hand
	Of yonder knight?
Servant	I know not, sir.
ROMEO	O, she doth teach the torches to burn bright!
	It seems she hangs upon the cheek of night
	Like a rich jewel in an Ethiop's ear —
	Beauty too rich for use, for earth too dear!
	So shows a snowy dove trooping with crows
	As yonder lady o'er her fellows shows.
	The measure done, I'll watch her place of stand
	And, touching hers, make blessed my rude hand.
	Did my heart love till now? Forswear it, sight!
	For I ne'er saw true beauty till this night.
TYBALT	This, by his voice, should be a Montague.
	Fetch me my rapier, boy. What, dares the slave
	Come hither, cover'd with an antic face,
	To fleer and scorn at our solemnity?
	Now, by the stock and honour of my kin,

凯普莱特族人	请坐,请坐,好兄弟,我们两人现在是跳不起来的了;您还记得我们最后一次戴着假面跳舞是在什么时候?

凯普莱特族人　这话说来也有三十年啦。

凯　普　莱　特　什么,兄弟!没有这么久,没有这么久;那是在路森修结婚的那年,大概离现在有二十五年模样,我们曾经跳过一次。

凯普莱特族人　不止了,不止了;大哥,他的儿子也有三十岁啦。

凯　普　莱　特　我难道不知道吗?他的儿子两年以前还没有成年哩。

罗　密　欧　(向仆人)搀着那位骑士的手的那位小姐是谁?

仆　　　人　我不知道,先生。

罗　密　欧　啊!火炬远不及她的明亮;她皎然悬在暮天的颊上,像黑奴耳边璀璨的珠环;她是天上明珠降落人间!瞧她随着女伴进退周旋,像鸦群中一头白鸽翩跹。我要等舞阑后追随左右,握一握她那纤纤的素手。我从前的恋爱是假非真,今晚才遇见绝世的佳人!

提　伯　尔　特　听这个人的声音,好像是一个蒙太古家里的人。孩子,拿我的剑来。哼!这不知死活的奴才,竟敢套着一个鬼脸,到这儿来嘲笑我们的盛会吗?为了保持凯普莱

	To strike him dead I hold it not a sin.
CAPULET	Why, how now, kinsman? Wherefore storm you so?
TYBALT	Uncle, this is a Montague, our foe;
	A villain, that is hither come in spite
	To scorn at our solemnity this night.
CAPULET	Young Romeo is it?
TYBALT	'Tis he, that villain Romeo.
CAPULET	Content thee, gentle coz, let him alone.
	'A bears him like a portly gentleman,
	And, to say truth, Verona brags of him
	To be a virtuous and well-govern'd youth.
	I would not for the wealth of all this town
	Here in my house do him disparagement.
	Therefore be patient, take no note of him.
	It is my will; the which if thou respect,
	Show a fair presence and put off these frowns,
	An ill-beseeming semblance for a feast.
TYBALT	It fits when such a villain is a guest.
	I'll not endure him.
CAPULET	He shall be endur'd.
	What, goodman boy? I say he shall. Go to!
	Am I the master here, or you? Go to!
	You'll not endure him? God shall mend my soul!
	You'll make a mutiny among my guests!
	You will set cock-a-hoop! you'll be the man!
TYBALT	Why, uncle, 'tis a shame.
CAPULET	Go to, go to!
	You are a saucy boy. Is't so, indeed?
	This trick may chance to scathe you. I know what.

特家族的光荣，我把他杀死了也不算罪过。

凯普莱特 哎哟，怎么，侄儿！你怎么动起怒来啦？

提伯尔特 姑父，这是我们的仇家蒙太古家里的人；这贼子今天晚上到这儿来，一定不怀好意，存心来捣乱我们的盛会。

凯普莱特 他是罗密欧那小子吗？

提伯尔特 正是他，正是罗密欧这小杂种。

凯普莱特 别生气，好侄儿，让他去吧。瞧他的举动倒也规规矩矩；说句老实话，在维罗纳城里，他也算得一个品行很好的青年。我无论如何不愿意在我自己的家里跟他闹事。你还是耐着性子，别理他吧。我的意思就是这样，你要是听我的话，赶快收下了怒容，和和气气的，不要打断大家的兴致。

提伯尔特 这样一个贼子也来做我们的宾客，我怎么不生气？我不能容他在这儿放肆。

凯普莱特 不容也得容；哼，目无尊长的孩子！我偏要容他。嘿！谁是这里的主人？是你还是我？嘿！你容不得他！什么话！你要当着这些客人的面前吵闹吗？你不服气！你要充好汉！

提伯尔特 姑父，咱们不能忍受这样的耻辱。

凯普莱特 得啦，得啦，你真是一点规矩都不懂。——是真的吗？

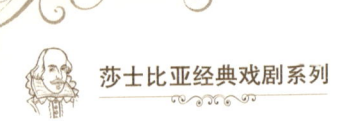

	You must contrary me! Marry, 'tis time —
	Well said, my hearts! — You are a princox — go!
	Be quiet, or — More light, more light! — For shame!
	I'll make you quiet; what! — Cheerly, my hearts!
TYBALT	Patience perforce with wilful choler meeting
	Makes my flesh tremble in their different greeting.
	I will withdraw; but this intrusion shall,
	Now seeming sweet, convert to bitt'rest gall.
	[*Exit.*]
ROMEO	[*To Juliet.*] If I profane with my unworthiest hand
	This holy shrine, the gentle fine is this;
	My lips, two blushing pilgrims, ready stand
	To smooth that rough touch with a tender kiss.
JULIET	Good pilgrim, you do wrong your hand too much,
	Which mannerly devotion shows in this;
	For saints have hands that pilgrims' hands do touch,
	And palm to palm is holy palmers' kiss.
ROMEO	Have not saints lips, and holy palmers too?
JULIET	Ay, pilgrim, lips that they must use in pray'r.
ROMEO	O, then, dear saint, let lips do what hands do!
	They pray; grant thou, lest faith turn to despair.
JULIET	Saints do not move, though grant for prayers' sake.
ROMEO	Then move not while my prayer's effect I take.
	Thus from my lips, by thine my sin is purg'd. [*Kisses her.*]
JULIET	Then have my lips the sin that they have took.
ROMEO	Sin from my lips? O trespass sweetly urg'd!
	Give me my sin again. [*Kisses her.*]
JULIET	You kiss by th' book.

您也许不喜欢这个调调儿。——我知道你一定要跟我闹别扭!——说得很好,我的好人儿!——你是个放肆的孩子;去,别闹!不然的话——把灯再点亮些!把灯再点亮些!——不害臊的!我要叫你闭嘴。——啊!痛痛快快地玩一下,我的好人儿们!

提伯尔特 我这满腔怒火偏给他浇下一盆冷水,好教我气得浑身哆嗦。我且退下去;可是今天由他闯进了咱们的屋子,看他不会有一天得意反成后悔。(下)

罗 密 欧 (向朱丽叶)
要是我这俗手上的尘污,
亵渎了你的神圣的庙宇,
这两片嘴唇,含羞的信徒,
愿意用一吻乞求你宥恕。

朱 丽 叶 信徒,莫把你的手儿侮辱,
这样才是最虔诚的礼敬;
神明的手本许信徒接触,
掌心的密合远胜如亲吻。

罗 密 欧 生下了嘴唇有什么用处?

朱 丽 叶 信徒的嘴唇要祷告神明。

罗 密 欧 那么我要祈求你的允许,
让手的工作交给了嘴唇。

朱 丽 叶 你的祷告已蒙神明允准。

罗 密 欧 神明,请容我把殊恩受领。(吻朱丽叶)
这一吻涤清了我的罪孽。

朱 丽 叶 你的罪却沾上我的唇间。

罗 密 欧 啊,我的唇间有罪?感谢你精心的指摘!让我收回吧。
(吻朱丽叶)

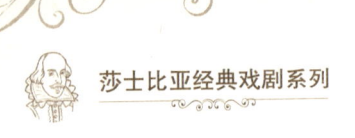

Nurse	Madam, your mother craves a word with you.
ROMEO	What is her mother?
Nurse	Marry, bachelor,
	Her mother is the lady of the house,
	And a good lady, and a wise and virtuous.
	I nurs'd her daughter that you talk'd withal.
	I tell you, he that can lay hold of her
	Shall have the chinks.
ROMEO	Is she a Capulet?
	O dear account! my life is my foe's debt.
BENVOLIO	Away, be gone; the sport is at the best.
ROMEO	Ay, so I fear; the more is my unrest.
CAPULET	Nay, gentlemen, prepare not to be gone;
	We have a trifling foolish banquet towards.
	Is it e'en so? Why then, I thank you all.
	I thank you, honest gentlemen. Good night.
	More torches here! [*Exeunt Maskers.*] Come on then, let's to bed.
	Ah, sirrah, by my fay, it waxes late;
	I'll to my rest.
	[*Exeunt all but Juliet and Nurse.*]
JULIET	Come hither, nurse. What is yond gentleman?
Nurse	The son and heir of old Tiberio.
JULIET	What's he that now is going out of door?
Nurse	Marry, that, I think, be young Petruchio.
JULIET	What's he that follows there, that would not dance?
Nurse	I know not.
JULIET	Go ask his name. — If he be married,
	My grave is like to be my wedding bed.

朱丽叶	你可以吻一下《圣经》。
乳母	小姐,你妈要跟你说话。
罗密欧	谁是她的母亲?
乳母	小官人,她的母亲就是这儿府上的太太,她是个好太太,又聪明,又贤德;我替她抚养她的女儿,就是刚才跟您说话的那个;告诉您吧,谁要是娶了她去,才发财啦。
罗密欧	她是凯普莱特家里的人吗?哎哟!我的生死现在操在我的仇人的手里了!
班伏里奥	去吧,跳舞快要完啦。
罗密欧	是的,我只怕盛筵易散,良会难逢。
凯普莱特	不,列位,请慢点儿去;我们还要请你们稍微用一点茶点。真要走吗?那么谢谢你们;各位朋友,谢谢,谢谢,再会!再会!再拿几个火把来!(持火把者下)来,我们去睡吧。啊,好小子!天真是不早了,我要去休息一会儿。(除朱丽叶及乳母外俱下)
朱丽叶	过来,奶妈。那边的那位绅士是谁?
乳母	提伯里奥那老头儿的儿子。
朱丽叶	现在跑出去的那个人是谁?
乳母	呃,我想他就是那个年轻的彼特鲁乔。
朱丽叶	那个跟在人家后面不跳舞的人是谁?
乳母	我不认识。
朱丽叶	去问他叫什么名字。——要是他已经结过婚,那么坟

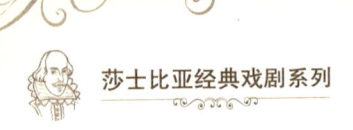

Nurse His name is Romeo, and a Montague,
The only son of your great enemy.

JULIET My only love, sprung from my only hate!
Too early seen unknown, and known too late!
Prodigious birth of love it is to me
That I must love a loathed enemy.

Nurse What's this? what's this?

JULIET A rhyme I learnt even now
Of one I danc'd withal.
[*One calls within, 'Juliet.'*]

Nurse Anon, anon!
Come, let's away; the strangers all are gone.
[*Exeunt.*]

|朱　丽　叶|墓便是我的婚床。|

乳　　　母	他的名字叫罗密欧，是蒙太古家里的人，咱们仇家的独子。
朱　丽　叶	恨灰中燃起了爱火融融， 要是不该相识，何必相逢！ 昨天的仇敌，今日的情人， 这场恋爱怕要种下祸根。
乳　　　母	你在说什么？你在说什么？
朱　丽　叶	那是刚才一个陪我跳舞的人教给我的几句诗。（内呼，"朱丽叶！"）
乳　　　母	就来，就来！来，咱们去吧；客人们都已经散了。（同下）

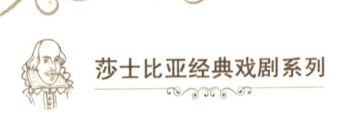

PROLOGUE

[*Enter Chorus.*]

Now old desire doth in his death bed lie,

And young affection gapes to be his heir;

That fair for which love groan'd for and would die,

With tender Juliet match'd, is now not fair.

Now Romeo is belov'd, and loves again,

Alike bewitched by the charm of looks;

But to his foe suppos'd he must complain,

And she steal love's sweet bait from fearful hooks.

Being held a foe, he may not have access

To breathe such vows as lovers use to swear,

And she as much in love, her means much less

To meet her new beloved anywhere;

But passion lends them power, time means, to meet,

Temp'ring extremities with extreme sweet.

[*Exit.*]

开场诗

（致辞者上念）

旧日的温情已尽付东流，
新生的爱恋正如日初上；
为了朱丽叶的绝世温柔，
忘却了曾为谁魂思梦想。
罗密欧爱着她媚人容貌，
把一片痴心呈献给仇雠；
朱丽叶恋着他风流才调，
甘愿被香饵钓上了金钩。
只恨解不开的世仇宿怨，
这段山海深情向谁申诉？
幽闺中锁住了桃花人面，
要相见除非是梦魂来去。
可是热情总会战胜辛艰，
苦味中间才有无限甘甜。（下）

Act II

SCENE I Verona. A lane by the wall of Capulet's orchard.

[*Enter Romeo alone.*]

ROMEO Can I go forward when my heart is here?
Turn back, dull earth, and find thy centre out.
[*Climbs the wall and leaps doun within it.*]
[*Enter Benvolio with Mercutio.*]

BENVOLIO Romeo! my cousin Romeo! Romeo!

MERCUTIO He is wise,
And, on my life, hath stol'n him home to bed.

BENVOLIO He ran this way, and leapt this orchard wall.
Call, good Mercutio.

MERCUTIO Nay, I'll conjure too.
Romeo! humours! madman! passion! lover!
Appear thou in the likeness of a sigh;
Speak but one rhyme, and I am satisfied!
Cry but 'Ay me!' pronounce but 'love' and 'dove';
Speak to my gossip Venus one fair word,
One nickname for her purblind son and heir,
Young Adam Cupid, he that shot so trim
When King Cophetua lov'd the beggar maid!
He heareth not, he stirreth not, he moveth not;
The ape is dead, and I must conjure him.
I conjure thee by Rosaline's bright eyes.
By her high forehead and her scarlet lip,

第二幕

第一场　维罗纳。凯普莱特花园
　　　　　墙外的小巷

（罗密欧上）

罗　密　欧　我的心还逗留在这里，我能够就这样掉头前去吗？转回去，你这无精打采的身子，去找寻你的灵魂吧。（攀登墙上，跳入墙内）

（班伏里奥及茂丘西奥上）

班伏里奥　罗密欧！罗密欧兄弟！

茂丘西奥　他是个乖巧的家伙；我说他一定溜回家去睡了。

班伏里奥　他往这条路上跑，一定跳进这花园的墙里去了。好茂丘西奥，你叫叫他吧。

茂丘西奥　不，我还要念咒喊他出来呢。罗密欧！痴人！疯子！恋人！情郎！快快化作一声叹息出来吧！我不要你多说什么，只要你念一行诗，叹一口气，把咱们那位维纳斯奶奶恭维两句，替她的瞎眼儿子丘比特少爷取个绰号，这位小爱神真是个神弓手，竟让国王爱上了叫花子的女儿！他没有听见，他没有作声，他没有动静；这猴崽子难道死了吗？待我咒他的鬼魂出来。凭着罗瑟琳的光明的眼睛，凭着她的高额角，她的红嘴唇，她的玲珑的脚、挺直的小腿、弹性的大腿

| | By her fine foot, straight leg, and quivering thigh, |
| And the demesnes that there adjacent lie, |
| That in thy likeness thou appear to us! |

BENVOLIO An if he hear thee, thou wilt anger him.

MERCUTIO This cannot anger him. 'Twould anger him
To raise a spirit in his mistress' circle
Of some strange nature, letting it there stand
Till she had laid it and conjur'd it down.
That were some spite; my invocation
Is fair and honest: in his mistress' name,
I conjure only but to raise up him.

BENVOLIO Come, He hath hid himself among these trees
To be consorted with the humorous night.
Blind is his love and best befits the dark.

MERCUTIO If love be blind, love cannot hit the mark.
Now will he sit under a medlar tree
And wish his mistress were that kind of fruit
As maids call medlars when they laugh alone.
O, Remeo, that she were, O that she were
An open et cetera, thou a pop'rin pear!
Remeo, goodnight. I'll to my truckle-bed;
This field-bed is too cold for me to sleep.
Come, shall we go?

BENVOLIO Go then, for 'tis in vain
To seek him here that means not to be found.
[*Exeunt.*]

和大腿附近的那一部分，凭着这一切的名义，赶快给我现出真形来吧！

班伏里奥 他要是听见了，一定会生气的。

茂丘西奥 这不至于叫他生气；他要是生气，除非是气得他在他情人的圈儿里唤起一个异样的妖精，由它在那儿昂然直立，直等她降伏了它，并使它低下头来；那样做的话，才是怀着恶意呢；我的咒语却很正当，我无非凭着他情人的名字唤他出来罢了。

班伏里奥 来，他已经躲到树丛里，跟那多露水的黑夜作伴去了；爱情本来是盲目的，让他在黑暗里摸索去吧。

茂丘西奥 爱情如果是盲目的，就射不中靶。此刻他该坐在枇杷树下了，希望他的情人就是他口中的枇杷。——啊，罗密欧，但愿，但愿她真的成了你到口的枇杷！罗密欧，晚安！我要上床睡觉去；这儿草地上太冷啦，我可受不了。来，咱们走吧。

班伏里奥 好，走吧；他要避着我们，找他也是白费辛勤。（同下）

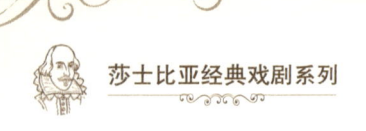

SCENE II *The same. Capulet's orchard.*

[*Enter Romeo.*]

ROMEO He jests at scars that never felt a wound.

[*Enter Juliet above at a window.*]

But soft! What light through yonder window breaks?
It is the East, and Juliet is the sun!
Arise, fair sun, and kill the envious moon,
Who is already sick and pale with grief
That thou her maid art far more fair than she.
Be not her maid, since she is envious.
Her vestal livery is but sick and green,
And none but fools do wear it. Cast it off.
It is my lady; O, it is my love!
O that she knew she were!
She speaks, yet she says nothing. What of that?
Her eye discourses; I will answer it.
I am too bold; 'tis not to me she speaks.
Two of the fairest stars in all the heaven,
Having some business, do entreat her eyes
To twinkle in their spheres till they return.
What if her eyes were there, they in her head?
The brightness of her cheek would shame those stars
As daylight doth a lamp; her eyes in heaven
Would through the airy region stream so bright
That birds would sing and think it were not night.
See how she leans her cheek upon her hand!
O that I were a glove upon that hand,

第二场　同前。凯普莱特家的花园

（罗密欧上）

罗密欧　没有受过伤的才会讥笑别人身上的创痕。（朱丽叶自上方窗户中出现）轻声！那边窗子里亮起来的是什么光？那就是东方，朱丽叶就是太阳！起来吧，美丽的太阳！赶走那妒忌的月亮，她因为她的女弟子比她美得多，已经气得面色惨白了。既然她这样妒忌着你，你不要忠于她吧；脱下她给你的这一身惨绿色的贞女的道服，它是只配给愚人穿的。那是我的意中人；啊！那是我的爱；唉，但愿她知道我在爱着她！她欲言又止，可是她的眼睛已经道出了她的心事。待我去回答她吧；不，我不要太鲁莽，她不是对我说话。天上两颗最灿烂的星，因为有事他去，请求她的眼睛替代它们在空中闪耀。要是她的眼睛变成了天上的星，天上的星变成了她的眼睛，那便怎样呢？她脸上的光辉会掩盖了星星的明亮，正像灯光在朝阳下黯然失色一样；在天上的她的眼睛，会在太空中大放光明，使鸟儿误认为黑夜已经过去而唱出它们的歌声。瞧！她用纤手托住了脸，那姿态是多么美妙！啊，但愿我是那一只手上

	That I might touch that cheek!
JULIET	Ay me!
ROMEO	She speaks.
	O, speak again, bright angel! for thou art
	As glorious to this night, being o'er my head,
	As is a winged messenger of heaven
	Unto the white-upturned wond'ring eyes
	Of mortals that fall back to gaze on him
	When he bestrides the lazy-pacing clouds
	And sails upon the bosom of the air.
JULIET	O Romeo, Romeo! wherefore art thou Romeo?
	Deny thy father and refuse thy name;
	Or, if thou wilt not, be but sworn my love,
	And I'll no longer be a Capulet.
ROMEO	[*Aside.*] Shall I hear more, or shall I speak at this?
JULIET	'Tis but thy name that is my enemy.
	Thou art thyself, though not a Montague.
	What's Montague? it is nor hand, nor foot,
	Nor arm, nor face, nor any other part
	Belonging to a man. O, be some other name!
	What's in a name? That which we call a rose
	By my other name would smell as sweet.
	So Romeo would, were he not Romeo call'd,
	Retain that dear perfection which he owes
	Without that title. Romeo, doff thy name;
	And for that name, which is no part of thee,
	Take all myself.
ROMEO	I take thee at thy word.
	Call me but love, and I'll be new baptiz'd;

的手套，好让我亲一亲她脸上的香泽！

朱丽叶　唉！

罗密欧　她说话了。啊！再说下去吧，光明的天使！因为我在这夜色之中仰视着你，就像一个尘世的凡人，张大了出神的眼睛，瞻望着一个生着翅膀的天使，驾着白云缓缓地驰过了天空一样。

朱丽叶　罗密欧啊，罗密欧！为什么你偏偏是罗密欧呢？否认你的父亲，抛弃你的姓名吧；也许你不愿意这样做，那么只要你宣誓做我的爱人，我也不愿再姓凯普莱特了。

罗密欧　（旁白）我是继续听下去呢，还是现在就对她说话？

朱丽叶　只有你的名字才是我的仇敌；你即使不姓蒙太古，仍然是这样的一个你。姓不姓蒙太古又有什么关系呢？它又不是手，又不是脚，又不是手臂，又不是脸，又不是身体上任何其他的部分。啊！换一个姓名吧！姓名本来是没有意义的；我们叫作玫瑰的这一种花，要是换了个名字，它的香味还是同样的芬芳；罗密欧要是换了别的名字，他的可爱的完美也决不会有丝毫改变。罗密欧，抛弃了你的名字吧；我愿意把我整个的心灵，赔偿你这一个身外的空名。

罗密欧　那么我就听你的话，你只要称我为爱，我就重新受洗，

	Henceforth I never will be Romeo.
JULIET	What man art thou that, thus bescreen'd in night, So stumblest on my counsel?
ROMEO	By a name I know not how to tell thee who I am. My name, dear saint, is hateful to myself, Because it is an enemy to thee. Had I it written, I would tear the word.
JULIET	My ears have yet not drunk a hundred words Of that tongue's utteronce, yet I know the sound. Art thou not Romeo, and a Montague?
ROMEO	Neither, fair saint, if either thee dislike.
JULIET	How cam'st thou hither, tell me, and wherefore? The orchard walls are high and hard to climb, And the place death, considering who thou art, If any of my kinsmen find thee here.
ROMEO	With love's light wings did I o'erperch these walls; For stony limits cannot hold love out, And what love can do, that dares love attempt. Therefore thy kinsmen are no stop to me.
JULIET	If they do see thee, they will murther thee.
ROMEO	Alack, there lies more peril in thine eye Than twenty of their swords! Look thou but sweet, And I am proof against their enmity.
JULIET	I would not for the world they saw thee here.
ROMEO	I have night's cloak to hide me from their eyes; And but thou love me, let them find me here. My life were better ended by their hate Than death prorogued, wanting of thy love.

罗密欧与朱丽叶
ROMEO AND JULIET

重新命名；从今以后，永远不再叫罗密欧了。

朱丽叶　你是什么人，在黑夜里躲躲闪闪地偷听人家的话？

罗密欧　我没法告诉你我叫什么名字。敬爱的神明，我痛恨我自己的名字，因为它是你的仇敌；要是把它写在纸上，我一定把这几个字撕成粉碎。

朱丽叶　我的耳朵里还没有灌进从你嘴里吐出来的一百个字，可是我认识你的声音；你不是罗密欧——蒙太古家里的人吗？

罗密欧　不是，美人，要是你不喜欢这两个名字。

朱丽叶　告诉我，你怎么会到这儿来，为什么到这儿来？花园的墙这么高，是不容易爬上来的；要是我家里的人瞧见你在这儿，他们一定不让你活命。

罗密欧　我借着爱的轻翼飞过园墙，因为砖石的墙垣是不能把爱情阻隔的；爱情的力量所能够做到的事，它都会冒险尝试，所以我不怕你家里人的干涉。

朱丽叶　要是他们瞧见了你，一定会把你杀死的。

罗密欧　唉！你的眼睛比他们二十柄刀剑还厉害；只要你用温柔的眼光看着我，他们就不能伤害我的身体。

朱丽叶　我怎么也不愿让他们瞧见你在这儿。

罗密欧　朦胧的夜色可以替我遮过他们的眼睛。只要你爱我，就让他们瞧见我吧；与其因为得不到你的爱情而在这世上捱命，还不如在仇人的刀剑下丧生。

JULIET	By whose direction found'st thou out this place?
ROMEO	By love, that first did prompt me to enquire.
	He lent me counsel, and I lent him eyes.
	I am no pilot; yet, wert thou as far
	As that vast shore wash'd with the farthest sea,
	I should adventure for such merchandise.
JULIET	Thou knowest the mask of night is on my face;
	Else would a maiden blush bepaint my cheek
	For that which thou hast heard me speak to-night.
	Fain would I dwell on form—fain, fain deny
	What I have spoke; but farewell compliment!
	Dost thou love me? I know thou wilt say 'Ay';
	And I will take thy word. Yet, if thou swear'st,
	Thou mayst prove false. At lovers' perjuries,
	They say Jove laughs. O gentle Romeo,
	If thou dost love, pronounce it faithfully.
	Or if thou thinkest I am too quickly won,
	I'll frown, and be perverse, and say thee nay,
	So thou wilt woo; but else, not for the world.
	In truth, fair Montague, I am too fond,
	And therefore thou mayst think my haviour light;
	But trust me, gentleman, I'll prove more true
	Than those that have more cunning to be strange.
	I should have been more strange, I must confess,
	But that thou overheard'st, ere I was ware,
	My true-love passion. Therefore pardon me,
	And not impute this yielding to light love,
	Which the dark night hath so discovered.
ROMEO	Lady, by yonder blessed moon I vow,

朱丽叶 谁叫你找到这儿来的?

罗密欧 爱情怂恿我探听出这一个地方;他替我出主意,我借给他眼睛。我不会操舟驾舵,可是倘使你在辽远辽远的海滨,我也会冒着风波寻访你这颗珍宝。

朱丽叶 幸亏黑夜替我罩上了一重面幕,否则为了我刚才被你听去的话,你一定可以看见我脸上羞愧的红晕。我真想遵守礼法,否认已经说过的言语,可是这些虚文俗礼,现在只好一切置之不顾了!你爱我吗?我知道你一定会说"是的";我也一定会相信你的话;可是也许你起的誓只是一个谎,人家说,对于恋人们的寒盟背信,天神是一笑置之的。温柔的罗密欧啊!你要是真的爱我,就请你诚意告诉我;你要是嫌我太容易降心相从,我也会堆起怒容,装出倔强的神气,拒绝你的好意,好让你向我婉转求情,否则我是无论如何不会拒绝你的。俊秀的蒙太古啊,我真的太痴心了,所以也许你会觉得我的举动有点轻浮;可是相信我,朋友,总有一天你会知道我的忠心远胜过那些善于矜持作态的人。我必须承认,倘不是你乘我不备的时候偷听去了我的真情的表白,我一定会更加矜持一点的;所以原谅我吧,是黑夜泄漏了我心底的秘密,不要把我的允诺看作无耻的轻狂。

罗密欧 姑娘,凭着这一轮皎洁的月亮,它的银光涂染着这些

	That tips with silver all these fruit-tree tops —
JULIET	O, swear not by the moon, th' inconstant moon,
	That monthly changes in her circled orb,
	Lest that thy love prove likewise variable.
ROMEO	What shall I swear by?
JULIET	Do not swear at all;
	Or if thou wilt, swear by thy gracious self,
	Which is the god of my idolatry,
	And I'll believe thee.
ROMEO	If my heart's dear love —
JULIET	Well, do not swear. Although I joy in thee,
	I have no joy of this contract to-night.
	It is too rash, too unadvis'd, too sudden;
	Too like the lightning, which doth cease to be
	Ere one can say 'It lightens.' Sweet, goodnight!
	This bud of love, by summer's ripening breath,
	May prove a beauteous flow'r when next we meet.
	Goodnight, goodnight! As sweet repose and rest
	Come to thy heart as that within my breast!
ROMEO	O, wilt thou leave me so unsatisfied?
JULIET	What satisfaction canst thou have to-night?
ROMEO	Th' exchange of thy love's faithful vow for mine.
JULIET	I gave thee mine before thou didst request it;
	And yet I would it were to give again.
ROMEO	Would'st thou withdraw it? For what purpose, love?
JULIET	But to be frank and give it thee again.
	And yet I wish but for the thing I have.
	My bounty is as boundless as the sea,
	My love as deep; the more I give to thee,

果树的梢端,我发誓——

朱丽叶 啊!不要指着月亮起誓,它是变化无常的,每个月都有盈亏圆缺;你要是指着它起誓,也许你的爱情也会像它一样无常。

罗密欧 那么我指着什么起誓呢?

朱丽叶 不用起誓吧;或者要是你愿意的话,就凭着你优美的自身起誓,那是我所崇拜的偶像,我一定会相信你的。

罗密欧 要是我的出自深心的爱情——

朱丽叶 好,别起誓啦。我虽然喜欢你,却不喜欢今天晚上的密约;它太仓卒、太轻率、太出人意外了,正像一闪电光,等不及人家开一声口,已经消隐了下去。好人,再会吧!这一朵爱的蓓蕾,靠着夏天的暖风的吹拂,也许会在我们下次相见的时候,开出鲜艳的花来。晚安,晚安!但愿恬静的安息同样降临到你我两人的心头!

罗密欧 啊!你就这样离我而去,不给我一点满足吗?

朱丽叶 你今夜还要什么满足呢?

罗密欧 你还没有把你的爱情的忠实的盟誓跟我交换。

朱丽叶 在你没有要求以前,我已经把我的爱给了你了;可是我倒愿意重新给你。

罗密欧 你要把它收回去吗?为什么呢,爱人?

朱丽叶 为了表示我的慷慨,我要把它重新给你。可是我只愿意要我已有的东西:我的慷慨像海一样浩渺,我的爱情也像海一样深沉;我给你的越多,我自己也越是富有,

	The more I have, for both are infinite.I hear some noise within. Dear love, adieu!
	[*Murse calls within.*]
	Anon, good nurse! Sweet Montague, be true.
	Stay but a little, I will come again. [*Exit.*]
ROMEO	O blessed, blessed night! I am afeared,
	Being in night, all this is but a dream,
	Too flattering-sweet to be substantial.
	[*Enter Juliet above.*]
JULIET	Three words, dear Romeo, and good night indeed.
	If that thy bent of love be honourable,
	Thy purpose marriage, send me word to-morrow,
	By one that I'll procure to come to thee,
	Where and what time thou wilt perform the rite;
	And all my fortunes at thy foot I'll lay
	And follow thee my lord throughout the world.
Nurse	[*Within.*] Madam!
JULIET	I come, anon.— But if thou meanest not well,
	I do beseech thee—
Nurse	[*Within.*] Madam!
JULIET	By-and-by I come.—
	To cease thy suit and leave me to my grief.
	To-morrow will I send.
ROMEO	So thrive my soul—
JULIET	A thousand times good night!
	[*Exit.*]
ROMEO	A thousand times the worse, to want thy light!
	Love goes toward love as schoolboys from their books;
	But love from love, toward school with heavy looks.

因为这两者都是没有穷尽的。（乳母在内呼唤）我听见里面有人在叫；亲爱的，再会吧！——就来了，好奶妈！——亲爱的蒙太古，愿你不要负心。再等一会儿，我就会来的。（自上方下）

罗密欧　幸福的，幸福的夜啊！我怕我只是在晚上做了一个梦，这样美满的事不会是真实的。

（朱丽叶自上方重上）

朱丽叶　亲爱的罗密欧，再说三句话，我们真的要再会了。要是你的爱情的确是光明正大，你的目的是在于婚姻，那么明天我会叫一个人到你的地方来，请你叫他带一个信给我，告诉我你愿意在什么地方、什么时候举行婚礼；我就会把我的整个命运交托给你，把你当作我的主人，跟随你到天涯海角。

乳　母　（在内）小姐！

朱丽叶　就来。——可是你要是没有诚意，那么我请求你——

乳　母　（在内）小姐！

朱丽叶　等一等，我来了。——停止你的求爱，让我一个人独自伤心吧。明天我就叫人来看你。

罗密欧　凭着我的灵魂——

朱丽叶　一千次的晚安！（自上方下）

罗密欧　晚上没有你的光，我只有一千次的心伤！恋爱的人去赴他情人的约会，像一个放学归来的儿童；可是当他和情人分别的时候，却像上学去一般满脸懊丧。（退后）

[*Retires.*]

[*Enter Julieta gain, above.*]

JULIET Hist! Romeo, hist! O for a falconer's voice
To lure this tassel-gentle back again!
Bondage is hoarse and may not speak aloud,
Else would I tear the cave where Echo lies,
And make her airy tongue more hoarse than mine
With repetition of 'My Romeo!'

ROMEO It is my soul that calls upon my name.
How silver-sweet sound lovers' tongues by night,
Like softest music to attending ears!

JULIET Romeo?

ROMEO My dear?

JULIET At what o'clock to-morrow
Shall I send to thee?

ROMEO By the hour of nine.

JULIET I will not fail. 'Tis twenty years till then.
I have forgot why I did call thee back.

ROMEO Let me stand here till thou remember it.

JULIET I shall forget, to have thee still stand there,
Rememb'ring how I love thy company.

ROMEO And I'll still stay, to have thee still forget,
Forgetting any other home but this.

JULIET 'Tis almost morning. I would have thee gone —
And yet no farther than a wanton's bird,
That lets it hop a little from her hand,
Like a poor prisoner in his twisted gyves,
And with a silken thread plucks it back again,
So loving-jealous of his liberty.

罗密欧与朱丽叶
ROMEO AND JULIET

（朱丽叶自上方重上）

朱丽叶　嘘！罗密欧！嘘！唉！我希望我会发出呼鹰的声音，招这只鹰儿回来。我不能高声说话，否则我要让我的喊声传进厄科的洞穴，让她的无形的喉咙因为反复叫喊着我的罗密欧的名字而变得嘶哑。

罗密欧　那是我的灵魂在叫喊着我的名字。恋人的声音在晚间多么清婉，听上去就像最柔和的音乐！

朱丽叶　罗密欧！

罗密欧　我的爱！

朱丽叶　明天我应该在什么时候叫人来看你？

罗密欧　就在九点钟吧。

朱丽叶　我一定不失信；挨到那个时候，该有二十年那么长久！我记不起为什么要叫你回来了。

罗密欧　让我站在这儿，等你记起了告诉我。

朱丽叶　你这样站在我的面前，我一心想着多么爱跟你在一块儿，一定永远记不起来了。

罗密欧　那么我就永远等在这儿，让你永远记不起来，忘记除了这里以外还有什么家。

朱丽叶　天快要亮了；我希望你快去；可是我就好比一个淘气的女孩子，像放松一个囚犯似的让她心爱的鸟儿暂时跳出她的掌心，又用一根丝线把它拉了回来，爱的私心使她不愿意给它自由。

ROMEO	I would I were thy bird.
JULIET	Sweet, so would I.
	Yet I should kill thee with much cherishing.
	Good night, goodnight! Parting is such sweet sorrow,
	That I shall say goodnight till it be morrow.
	[*Exit.*]
ROMEO	Sleep dwell upon thine eyes, peace in thy breast!
	Would I were sleep and peace, so sweet to rest!
	Hence will I to my ghostly father's cell,
	His help to crave and my dear hap to tell.
	[*Exit.*]

SCENE III   *The same. Friar Laurence's cell.*

[*Enter Friar Laurence alone, with a basket.*]

Friar   The grey-ey'd morn smiles on the frowning night,
Check'ring the Eastern clouds with streaks of light;
And flecked darkness like a drunkard reels
From forth day's path and Titan's fiery wheels.
Now, ere the sun advance his burning eye
The day to cheer and night's dank dew to dry,
I must up-fill this osier cage of ours
With baleful weeds and precious-juiced flowers.
The earth that's nature's mother is her tomb.
What is her burying grave, that is her womb;
And from her womb children of divers kind
We sucking on her natural bosom find,
Many for many virtues excellent,

罗密欧　　我但愿我是你的鸟儿。
朱丽叶　　好人,我也但愿这样;可是我怕你会死在我的过分的爱抚里。晚安!晚安!离别是这样甜蜜的凄清,我真要向你道晚安直到天明!(下)
罗密欧　　但愿睡眠合上你的眼睛!
　　　　　但愿平静安息我的心灵!
　　　　　我如今要去向神父求教,
　　　　　把今宵的艳遇诉他知晓。(下)

第三场　同前。劳伦斯神父的寺院

(劳伦斯神父携篮上)

劳伦斯　　黎明笑向着含愠的残宵,
　　　　　金鳞浮上了东方的天梢;
　　　　　看赤轮驱走了片片乌云,
　　　　　像一群醉汉向四处狼奔。
　　　　　趁太阳还没有睁开火眼,
　　　　　晒干深夜里的涔涔露点,
　　　　　我待要采摘下满篌盈筐,
　　　　　毒草灵葩充实我的青囊。
　　　　　大地是生化万类的慈母,
　　　　　她又是掩藏群生的坟墓,
　　　　　试看她无所不载的胸怀,
　　　　　哺乳着多少的姹女婴孩!
　　　　　天生下的万物没有弃掷,

None but for some, and yet all different.
O, mickle is the powerful grace that lies
In plants, herbs, stones, and their true qualities;
For naught so vile that on the earth doth live
But to the earth some special good doth give;
Nor aught so good but, strain'd from that fair use,
Revolts from true birth, stumbling on abuse.
Virtue itself turns vice, being misapplied,
And vice sometime's by action dignified.
[*Enter Romeo.*]
Within the infant rind of this weak flower
Poison hath residence, and medicine power;
For this, being smelt, with that part cheers each part;
Being tasted, stays all senses with the heart.
Two such opposed kings encamp them still
In man as well as herbs— grace and rude will;
And where the worser is predominant,
Full soon the canker death eats up that plant.

ROMEO Good morrow, father.

Friar Benedicite!
What early tongue so sweet saluteth me?
Young son, it argues a distempered head
So soon to bid good morrow to thy bed.
Care keeps his watch in every old man's eye,
And where care lodges sleep will never lie;
But where unbruised youth with unstuff'd brain
Doth couch his limbs, there golden sleep doth reign.
Therefore thy earliness doth me assure
Thou art uprous'd with some distemp'rature;

什么都有它各自的特色,
石块的冥顽,草木的无知,
都含着玄妙的造化生机。
莫看那蠢蠢的恶木莠蔓,
对世间都有它特殊贡献;
即使最纯良的美谷嘉禾,
用得失当也会害性戕躯。
美德的误用会变成罪过,
罪恶有时反会造成善果。

（罗密欧上）

这一朵有毒的弱蕊纤苞,
也会把淹煎的痼疾医疗;
它的香味可以祛除百病,
吃下腹中却会昏迷不醒。
草木和人心并没有不同,
各自有善意和恶念争雄;
恶的势力倘然占了上风,
死便会蛀蚀进它的心中。

罗密欧 早安,神父。

劳伦斯 上帝祝福你!是谁的温柔的声音这么早就在叫我?孩子,你一早起身,一定有什么心事。老年人因为多忧多虑,往往容易失眠,可是身心壮健的青年,一上了

	Or if not so, then here I hit it right —
	Our Romeo hath not been in bed to-night.
ROMEO	That last is true — the sweeter rest was mine.
Friar	God pardon sin! Wast thou with Rosaline?
ROMEO	With Rosaline? My ghostly father? no.
	I have forgot that name, and that name's woe.
Friar	That's my good son! But where hast thou been then?
ROMEO	I'll tell thee ere thou ask it me again.
	I have been feasting with mine enemy,
	Where on a sudden one hath wounded me
	That's by me wounded. Both our remedies
	Within thy help and holy physic lies.
	I bear no hatred, blessed man, for, lo,
	My intercession likewise steads my foe.
Friar	Be plain, good son, and homely in thy drift
	Riddling confession finds but riddling shrift.
ROMEO	Then plainly know my heart's dear love is set
	On the fair daughter of rich Capulet;
	As mine on hers, so hers is set on mine,
	And all combin'd, save what thou must combine
	By holy marriage. When, and where, and how
	We met, we woo'd, and made exchange of vow,
	I'll tell thee as we pass; but this I pray,
	That thou consent to marry us to-day.
Friar	Holy Saint Francis! What a change is here!
	Is Rosaline, that thou didst love so dear,
	So soon forsaken? Young men's love then lies
	Not truly in their hearts, but in their eyes.
	Jesu Maria! What a deal of brine

罗密欧与朱丽叶
ROMEO AND JULIET

床就应该酣然入睡；所以你的早起，倘不是因为有什么烦恼，一定是昨夜没有睡过觉。

罗密欧 你的第二个猜测是对的；我昨夜享受到比睡眠更甜蜜的安息。

劳伦斯 上帝饶恕我们的罪恶！你是跟罗瑟琳在一起吗？

罗密欧 跟罗瑟琳在一起，我的神父？不，我已经忘记了那一个名字和那个名字所带来的烦恼。

劳伦斯 那才是我的好孩子；可是你究竟到什么地方去了？

罗密欧 我愿意在你没有问我第二遍以前告诉你。昨天晚上我跟我的仇敌在一起宴会，突然有一个人伤害了我，同时她也被我伤害了；只有你的帮助和你的圣药，才会医治我们两人的重伤。神父，我并不怨恨我的敌人，因为瞧，我来向你请求的事，不单为了我自己，也同样为了她。

劳伦斯 好孩子，说明白一点，把你的意思老老实实告诉我，别打着哑谜了。

罗密欧 那么老实告诉你吧，我心底的一往深情，已经完全倾注在凯普莱特的美丽的女儿身上了。她也同样爱着我；一切都完全定当了，只要你肯替我们主持神圣的婚礼。我们在什么时候遇见，在什么地方求爱，怎样彼此交换着盟誓，这一切我都可以慢慢告诉你；可是无论如何，请你一定答应就在今天替我们成婚。

劳伦斯 圣芳济啊！多么快的变化！难道你所深爱着的罗瑟琳，就这样一下子被你抛弃了吗？这样看来，年轻人的爱

Hath wash'd thy sallow cheeks for Rosaline!
How much salt water thrown away in waste
To season love, that of it doth not taste!
The sun not yet thy sighs from heaven clears,
Thy old groans ring yet in mine ancient ears.
Lo, here upon thy cheek the stain doth sit
Of an old tear that is not wash'd off yet.
If e'er thou wast thyself, and these woes thine,
Thou and these woes were all for Rosaline.
And art thou chang'd? Pronounce this sentence then:
Women may fall when there's no strength in men.

ROMEO Thou chid'st me oft for loving Rosaline.

Friar For doting, not for loving, pupil mine.

ROMEO And bad'st me bury love.

Friar Not in a grave
To lay one in, another out to have.

ROMEO I pray thee chide me not. She whom I love now
Doth grace for grace and love for love allow.
The other did not so.

Friar O, she knew well
Thy love did read by rote, that could not spell.
But come, young waverer, come go with me.
In one respect I'll thy assistant be;
For this alliance may so happy prove
To turn your households' rancour to pure love.

ROMEO O, let us hence! I stand on sudden haste.

Friar Wisely, and slow. They stumble that run fast.

[*Exeunt.*]

情，都是见异思迁，不是发于真心的。耶稣，马利亚！你为了罗瑟琳的缘故，曾经用多少的眼泪洗过你消瘦的面庞！为了替无味的爱情添加一点辛酸的味道，曾经浪费掉多少的咸水！太阳还没有扫清你吐向苍穹的怨气，我这龙钟的耳朵里还留着你往日的呻吟！瞧！就在你自己的颊上，还剩着一丝不曾揩去的旧时的泪痕。要是你不曾变了一个人，这些悲哀都是你真实的情感，那么你是罗瑟琳的，这些悲哀也是为罗瑟琳而发的；难道你现在已经变心了吗？男人既然这样没有恒心，那就莫怪女人家朝三暮四了。

罗密欧　你常常因为我爱罗瑟琳而责备我。

劳伦斯　我的学生，我不是说你不该恋爱，我只叫你不要因为恋爱而发痴。

罗密欧　你又叫我把爱情埋葬在坟墓里。

劳伦斯　我没有叫你把旧的爱情埋葬了，再去另找新欢。

罗密欧　请你不要责备我；我现在所爱的她，跟我心心相印，不像前回那个一样。

劳伦斯　啊，罗瑟琳知道你对她的爱情完全抄着人云亦云的老调，你还没有读过恋爱入门的一课哩。可是来吧，朝三暮四的青年，跟我来；为了一个理由，我愿意帮助你一臂之力：因为你们的结合也许会使你们两家释嫌修好，那就是天大的幸事了。

罗密欧　啊！我们就去吧，我巴不得越快越好。

劳伦斯　凡事三思而行；跑得太快是会滑倒的。（同下）

SCENE IV *The same. A street.*

[*Enter Benvolio and Mercutio.*]

MERCUTIO Where the devil should this Romeo be?
Came he not home to-night?

BENVOLIO Not to his father's. I spoke with his man.

MERCUTIO Why, that same pale hard-hearted wench, that Rosaline,
Torments him so that he will sure run mad.

BENVOLIO Tybalt, the kinsman to old Capulet,
Hath sent a letter to his father's house.

MERCUTIO A challenge, on my life.

BENVOLIO Romeo will answer it.

MERCUTIO Any man that can write may answer a letter.

BENVOLIO Nay, he will answer the letter's master, how he dares, being dared.

MERCUTIO Alas, poor Romeo, he is already dead! stabb'd with a white wench's black eye; through the ear with a love song; the very pin of his heart cleft with the blind bow-boy's butt-shaft; and is he a man to encounter Tybalt?

BENVOLIO Why, what is Tybalt?

MERCUTIO More than Prince of Cats, I can tell you. O, he's the courageous captain of compliments. He fights as you sing pricksong — keeps time, distance, and proportion; rests me his minim rest, one, two, and the third in your bosom! the very butcher of a silk button, a duellist, a duellist! a gentleman of the very first house, of the first and second cause. Ah, the immortal passado! the punto

第四场 同前。街道

（班伏里奥及茂丘西奥上）

茂丘西奥　见鬼的,这罗密欧究竟到哪儿去了？他昨天晚上没有回家吗？

班伏里奥　没有,我问过他的仆人了。

茂丘西奥　哎哟！那个白面孔狠心肠的女人,那个罗瑟琳,一定把他虐待得要发疯了。

班伏里奥　提伯尔特,凯普莱特那老头子的亲戚,有一封信送到他父亲那里。

茂丘西奥　一定是一封挑战书。

班伏里奥　罗密欧一定会给他一个答复。

茂丘西奥　只要会写几个字,谁都会写一封复信。

班伏里奥　不,我说他一定会接受他的挑战。

茂丘西奥　唉！可怜的罗密欧！他已经死了,一个白女人的黑眼睛戳破了他的心；一支恋歌穿过了他的耳朵；瞎眼的丘比特的箭已把他当胸射中；他现在还能够抵得住提伯尔特吗？

班伏里奥　提伯尔特是个什么人？

茂丘西奥　我可以告诉你,他不是个平常的阿猫阿狗。啊！他是个胆大心细、剑法高明的人。他跟人打起架来,就像照着乐谱唱歌一样,一板一眼都不放松,一秒钟的停顿,然后一、二、三,刺进人家的胸膛；他全然是个穿礼服的屠夫,一个决斗的专家；一个名门贵胄,一个击剑能手。啊！那了不得的侧击！那反击！那直中要害

	reverso! the hay.
BENVOLIO	The what?
MERCUTIO	The pox of such antic, lisping, affecting fantasticoes — these new tuners of accent! 'By Jesu, a very good blade! a very tall man! a very good whore!' Why, is not this a lamentable thing, grandsir, that we should be thus afflicted with these strange flies, these fashion-mongers, these pardon-me's, who stand so much on the new form that they cannot sit at ease on the old bench? O, their bones, their bones!

[*Enter Romeo.*]

BENVOLIO	Here comes Romeo! here comes Romeo!
MERCUTIO	Without his roe, like a dried herring. O flesh, flesh, how art thou fishified! Now is he for the numbers that Petrarch flowed in. Laura, to his lady, was a kitchen wench (marry, she had a better love to berhyme her), Dido a dowdy, Cleopatra a gypsy, Helen and Hero hildings and harlots, Thisbe a gray eye or so, but not to the purpose. Signior Romeo, bon jour! There's a French salutation to your French slop. You gave us the counterfeit fairly last night.
ROMEO	Good morrow to you both. What counterfeit did I give you?
MERCUTIO	The slip, sir, the slip. Can you not conceive?
ROMEO	Pardon, good Mercutio. My business was great, and in such a case as mine a man may strain courtesy.
MERCUTIO	That's as much as to say, such a case as yours constrains a man to bow in the hams.
ROMEO	Meaning, to curtsy.

的一剑!

班伏里奥 那什么?

茂丘西奥 那些怪模怪样、扭扭捏捏的装腔作势,说起话来怪声怪气的荒唐鬼的对头。他们只会说,"耶稣哪,好一柄锋利的刀子!好一个高大的汉子,好一个风流的婊子!"嘿,我的老爷子,咱们中间有这么一群不知从哪儿飞来的苍蝇,这一群满嘴法国话的时髦人,他们因为趋新好异,坐在一张旧凳子上也会不舒服,这不是一件可以痛哭流涕的事吗?

(罗密欧上)

班伏里奥 罗密欧来了,罗密欧来了。

茂丘西奥 瞧他孤零零的神气,倒像一条风干的咸鱼。啊,你这块肉呀,你是怎样变成了鱼的!现在他又要念起彼特拉克的诗句来了:罗拉比起他的情人来不过是个灶下的丫头,虽然她有一个会作诗的爱人;狄多是个蓬头垢面的村妇;克莉奥佩屈拉是个吉卜赛姑娘;海伦、希罗都是下流的娼妓;提斯柏也许有一双美丽的灰色眼睛,可是也不配相提并论。罗密欧先生,给你个法国式的敬礼!昨天晚上你给我们开了多大的一个玩笑哪。

罗　密　欧 两位大哥早安!昨晚我开了什么玩笑?

茂丘西奥 你昨天晚上逃走得好;装什么假?

罗　密　欧 对不起,茂丘西奥,我当时有一件很重要的事情,在那情况下我只好失礼了。

茂丘西奥 这就是说,在那情况下,你不得不屈一屈膝了。

罗　密　欧 你的意思是说,赔个礼。

MERCUTIO	Thou hast most kindly hit it.
ROMEO	A most courteous exposition.
MERCUTIO	Nay, I am the very pink of courtesy.
ROMEO	Pink for flower.
MERCUTIO	Right.
ROMEO	Why, then is my pump well-flower'd.
MERCUTIO	Well said! Follow me this jest now till thou hast worn out thy pump, that, when the single sole of it is worn, the jest may remain, after the wearing, solely singular.
ROMEO	O single-soled jest, solely singular for the singleness!
MERCUTIO	Come between us, good Benvolio! My wits faints.
ROMEO	Swits and spurs, swits and spurs! or I'll cry a match.
MERCUTIO	Nay, if our wits run the wild-goose chase, I am done; for thou hast more of the wild goose in one of thy wits than, I am sure, I have in my whole five. Was I with you there for the goose?
ROMEO	Thou wast never with me for anything when thou wast not there for the goose.
MERCUTIO	I will bite thee by the ear for that jest.
ROMEO	Nay, good goose, bite not!
MERCUTIO	Thy wit is a very bitter sweeting; it is a most sharp sauce.
ROMEO	And is it not, then, well serv'd in to a sweet goose?
MERCUTIO	O, here's a wit of cheveril, that stretches from an inch narrow to an ell broad!
ROMEO	I stretch it out for that word 'broad', which, added to the goose, proves thee far and wide a broad goose.
MERCUTIO	Why, is not this better now than groaning for love? Now art thou sociable, now art thou Romeo; now art

茂丘西奥　你回答得正对。

罗密欧　正是十分有礼的说法。

茂丘西奥　何止如此,我是讲礼讲到头了。

罗密欧　像是花儿鞋子的尖头。

茂丘西奥　说得对。

罗密欧　那么我的鞋子已经全是花花的洞儿了。

茂丘西奥　讲得妙;跟着我把这个笑话追到底吧,直追得你的鞋子都破了,只剩下了鞋底,而那笑话也就变得又秃又呆了。

罗密欧　啊,好一个又呆又秃的笑话,真配傻子来说。

茂丘西奥　快来帮忙,好班伏里奥;我的脑袋不行了。

罗密欧　要来就快马加鞭;不然我就宣告胜利了。

茂丘西奥　不,如果比聪明像赛马,我承认我输了;我的马儿哪有你的野?说到野,我的五官加在一起也比不上你的任何一官。可是你野的时候,我几时跟你在一起过?

罗密欧　哪一次撒野没有你这呆头鹅?

茂丘西奥　你这话真有意思,我巴不得咬你一口才好。

罗密欧　啊,好鹅儿,莫咬我。

茂丘西奥　你的笑话又甜又辣;简直是好调料。

罗密欧　美鹅加调料,岂不绝妙?

茂丘西奥　啊,妙语横生,越拉越横!

罗密欧　横得好;你这呆头鹅变成一只横胖鹅了。

茂丘西奥　呀,我们这样打着趣岂不比呻吟求爱好得多吗?此刻

	thou what thou art, by art as well as by nature. For this drivelling love is like a great natural that runs lolling up and down to hide his bauble in a hole.
BENVOLIO	Stop there, stop there!
MERCUTIO	Thou desirest me to stop in my tale against the hair.
BENVOLIO	Thou wouldst else have made thy tale large.
MERCUTIO	O, thou art deceiv'd! I would have made it short; for I was come to the whole depth of my tale, and meant indeed to occupy the argument no longer.
ROMEO	Here's goodly gear!

[*Enter Nurse and her Man Peter.*]

MERCUTIO	A sail, a sail!
BENVOLIO	Two, two! a shirt and a smock.
Nurse	Peter!
PETER	Anon.
Nurse	My fan, PETER.
MERCUTIO	Good Peter, to hide her face; for her fan's the fairer face of the two.
Nurse	God ye good morrow, gentlemen.
MERCUTIO	God ye good-den, fair gentlewoman.
Nurse	Is it good-den?
MERCUTIO	'Tis no less, I tell ye; for the bawdy hand of the dial is now upon the prick of noon.
Nurse	Out upon you! What a man are you!
ROMEO	One, gentlewoman, that God hath made for himself to mar.
Nurse	By my troth, it is well said. 'For himself to mar,' quoth 'a? Gentlemen, can any of you tell me where I may find the young Romeo?

你多么和气，此刻你才真是罗密欧了；不论是先天还是后天，此刻是你的真面目了；为了爱，急得涕零满脸，就像一个天生的傻子，奔上奔下，找洞藏他的棍儿。

班伏里奥 打住吧，打住吧。

茂丘西奥 你不让我的话讲完，留着尾巴好不顺眼。

班伏里奥 不打住你，你的尾巴还要长大呢。

茂丘西奥 啊，你错了；我的尾巴本来就要缩小了；我的话已经讲到了底，不想老占着位置啦。

罗密欧 看哪，好把戏来啦！

（乳母及彼得上）

茂丘西奥 一条帆船，一条帆船！

班伏里奥 两条，两条！一公一母。

乳母 彼得！

彼得 有！

乳母 彼得，我的扇子。

茂丘西奥 好彼得，替她把脸遮了；因为她的扇子比她的脸好看一点。

乳母 早安，列位先生。

茂丘西奥 晚安，好太太。

乳母 是道晚安时候了吗？

茂丘西奥 我告诉你，不会错；那日晷上的指针正顶着中午呢。

乳母 你说什么！你是什么人！

罗密欧 好太太，上帝造了他，他可不知好歹。

乳母 说得好，你说他不知好歹哪？列位先生，你们有谁能够告诉我年轻的罗密欧在什么地方？

ROMEO	I can tell you; but young Romeo will be older when you have found him than he was when you sought him. I am the youngest of that name, for fault of a worse.
Nurse	You say well.
MERCUTIO	Yea, is the worst well? Very well took, i' faith! wisely, wisely!
Nurse	If you be he, sir, I desire some confidence with you.
BENVOLIO	She will indite him to some supper.
MERCUTIO	A bawd, a bawd, a bawd! So ho!
ROMEO	What hast thou found?
MERCUTIO	No hare, sir; unless a hare, sir, in a lenten pie, that is something stale and hoar ere it be spent. [*He walks by them and sings.*] 　An old hare hoar, 　And an old hare hoar, 　Is very good meat in Lent; 　But a hare that is hoar 　Is too much for a score 　When it hoars ere it be spent. Romeo, will you come to your father's? We'll to dinner thither.
ROMEO	I will follow you.
MERCUTIO	Farewell, ancient lady. Farewell, [*Sings.*] lady, lady, lady. [*Exeunt Mercutio, Benvolio.*]
Nurse	I Pray you, sir, what saucy merchant was this that was so full of his ropery?
ROMEO	A gentleman, Nurse, that loves to hear himself talk and will speak more in a minute than he will stand to in a month.

罗密欧与朱丽叶
ROMEO AND JULIET

罗　密　欧　我可以告诉你；可是等你找到他的时候，年轻的罗密欧已经比你寻访他的时候老了点儿了。我因为取不到一个好一点的名字，所以就叫作罗密欧；在取这一个名字的人们中间，我是最年轻的一个。

乳　　　母　您说得真好。

茂丘西奥　呀，这样一个最坏的家伙你也说好？想得周到；有道理，有道理。

乳　　　母　先生，要是您就是他，我要跟您单独讲句话儿。

班伏里奥　她要拉他吃晚饭去。

茂丘西奥　一个老虔婆，一个老虔婆！有了！有了！

罗　密　欧　有了什么？

茂丘西奥　不是什么野兔子；要说是兔子的话，也不过是斋节里做的兔肉饼，没有吃完就发了霉。（唱）

　　　　　老兔肉，发白霉，
　　　　　老兔肉，发白霉，
　　　　　原是斋节好点心；
　　　　　可是霉了的兔肉饼，
　　　　　二十个人也吃不尽，
　　　　　吃不完的霉肉饼。

罗密欧，你到不到你父亲那儿去？我们要在那边吃饭。

罗　密　欧　我就来。

茂丘西奥　再见，老太太；（唱）

再见，我的好姑娘！（茂丘西奥、班伏里奥下）

乳　　　母　好，再见！先生，这个满嘴胡说八道的放肆家伙是谁？

罗　密　欧　奶妈，这位先生最喜欢听他自己讲话；他在一分钟里所说的话，比他在一个月里听人家讲的话还多。

Nurse	And 'a speak anything against me, I'll take him down, an 'a were lustier than he is, and twenty such Jacks; and if I cannot, I'll find those that shall. Scurvy knave! I am none of his flirt-gills; I am none of his skains-mates. [*To Peter.*] And thou must stand by too, and suffer every knave to use me at his pleasure !
PETER	I saw no man use you at his pleasure. If I had, my weapon should quickly have been out, I warrant you. I dare draw as soon as another man, if I see occasion in a good quarrel, and the law on my side.
Nurse	Now, afore God, I am so vexed that every part about me quivers. Scurvy knave! Pray you, sir, a word; and, as I told you, my young lady bid me enquire you out. What she bid me say, I will keep to myself; but first let me tell ye, if ye should lead her into a fool's paradise, as they say, it were a very gross kind of behaviour, as they say; for the gentlewoman is young; and therefore, if you should deal double with her, truly it were an ill thing to be off'red to any gentlewoman, and very weak dealing.
ROMEO	Nurse, commend me to thy lady and mistress. I protest unto thee —
Nurse	Good heart, and i' faith I will tell her as much. Lord, Lord! she will be a joyful woman.
ROMEO	What wilt thou tell her, nurse? Thou dost not mark me.
Nurse	I will tell her, sir, that you do protest, which, as I take it, is a gentlemanlike offer.
ROMEO	Bid her devise Some means to come to shrift this afternoon;

罗密欧与朱丽叶
ROMEO AND JULIET

乳　母　要是他对我说了一句不客气的话，尽管他力气再大一点，我也要给他一顿教训；这种家伙二十个我都对付得了，要是对付不了，我会叫那些对付得了他们的人来。混账东西！他把老娘看作什么人啦？我不是那些烂污婊子，由他随便取笑。（向彼得）你也不是个好东西，看着人家把我欺侮，站在旁边一动也不动！

彼　得　我没有看见什么人欺侮你；要是我看见了，一定会立刻拔出刀子来的。碰到吵架的事，只要理直气壮，打起官司来不怕人家，我是从来不肯落在人家后头的。

乳　母　哎哟！真把我气得浑身发抖。混账的东西！对不起，先生，让我跟您说句话儿。我刚才说过的，我家小姐叫我来找您；她叫我说些什么话我可不能告诉您；可是我要先明白对您说一句，要是正像人家说的，您想骗她做一场春梦，那可真是人家说的一件顶坏的行为；因为这位姑娘年纪还小，所以您要是欺骗了她，实在是一桩对无论哪一位好人家的姑娘都是对不起的事情，而且也是一桩顶不应该的举动。

罗密欧　奶妈，请你替我向你家小姐致意。我可以对你发誓——

乳　母　很好，我就这样告诉她。主啊！主啊！她听见了一定会非常喜欢的。

罗密欧　奶妈，你去告诉她什么话呢？你没有听我说呀。

乳　母　我就对她说您发过誓了，证明您是一位正人君子。

罗密欧　你请她今天下午想个法子出来到劳伦斯神父的寺院里

	And there she shall at Friar Laurence' cell
	Be shriv'd and married. Here is for thy pains.
Nurse	No, truly, sir; not a penny.
ROMEO	Go to! I say you shall.
Nurse	This afternoon, sir? Well, she shall be there.
ROMEO	And stay, good nurse, behind the abbey wall.
	Within this hour my man shall be with thee
	And bring thee cords made like a tackled stair,
	Which to the high topgallant of my joy
	Must be my convoy in the secret night.
	Farewell. Be trusty, and I'll quit thy pains.
	Farewell. Commend me to thy mistress.
Nurse	Now God in heaven bless thee! Hark you, sir.
ROMEO	What say'st thou, my dear nurse?
Nurse	Is your man secret? Did you ne'er hear say,
	Two may keep counsel, putting one away?
ROMEO	I warrant thee my man's as true as steel.
Nurse	Well, sir, my mistress is the sweetest lady. Lord,Lord! when 'twas a little prating thing — O, there is a nobleman in town, one Paris, that would fain lay knife aboard; but she, good soul, had as lieve see a toad, a very toad, as see him. I anger her sometimes, and tell her that Paris is the properer man; but I'll warrant you, when I say so, she looks as pale as any clout in the versal world. Doth not rosemary and Romeo begin both with a letter?
ROMEO	Ay, Nurse; what of that? Both with an R.
Nurse	Ah, mocker! that's the dog's name. R is for the — No; I know it begins with some other letter; and she hath

忏悔，就在那个地方举行婚礼。这几个钱是给你的酬劳。

乳　　母　不，真的，先生，我一个钱也不要。

罗密欧　别客气了，你还是拿着吧。

乳　　母　今天下午吗，先生？好，她一定会去的。

罗密欧　好奶妈，请你在这寺墙后面等一等，就在这一点钟之内，我要叫我的仆人去拿一捆扎得像船上的软梯一样的绳子来给你带去；在秘密的夜里，我要凭着它攀登我的幸福的尖端。再会！愿你对我们忠心，我一定不会有负你的辛劳。再会！替我向你的小姐致意。

乳　　母　天上的上帝保佑您！先生，我对您说。

罗密欧　你有什么话说，我的好奶妈？

乳　　母　您那仆人可靠得住吗？您没听见古话说，两个人知道是秘密，三个人知道就不是秘密吗？

罗密欧　你放心吧，我的仆人是最可靠不过的。

乳　　母　好先生，我那小姐是个最可爱的姑娘——主啊！主啊！——那时候她还是个咿咿呀呀怪会说话的小东西——啊！本地有一位叫作帕里斯的贵人，他巴不得把我家小姐抢到手里；可是她，好人儿，瞧他比瞧一只蛤蟆还讨厌。我有时候对她说帕里斯人品不错，你才不知道哩，她一听见这样的话，就会气得面如土色。请问罗丝玛丽花和罗密欧是不是同样一个字开头的呀？

罗密欧　是呀，奶妈；怎么样？都是罗字起头的哪。

乳　　母　啊，你开玩笑哩！那是狗的名字啊；阿罗就是那个——不对；我知道一定是另一个字开头的——她还把你同

	the prettiest sententious of it, of you and rosemary, that it would do you good to hear it.
ROMEO	Commend me to thy lady.
Nurse	Ay, a thousand times. [*Exit Romeo.*] Peter!
PETER	Anon.
Nurse	Peter, take my fan, and go before, and apace.
	[*Exeunt.*]

SCENES V   The same. Capulet's orchard.

[*Enter Juliet.*]

JULIET	The clock struck nine when I did send the nurse;
	In half an hour she promis'd to return.
	Perchance she cannot meet him. That's not so.
	O, she is lame! Love's heralds should be thoughts,
	Which ten times faster glide than the sun's beams
	Driving back shadows over low'ring hills.
	Therefore do nimble-pinion'd doves draw Love,
	And therefore hath the wind-swift Cupid wings. ·
	Now is the sun upon the highmost hill
	Of this day's journey, and from nine till twelve
	Is three long hours; yet she is not come.
	Had she affections and warm youthful blood,
	She would beas swift in motion as a ball;
	My words would bandy her to my sweet love,
	And his to me,
	But old folks, many feign as they were dead —
	Unwieldy, slow, heavy and pale as lead.
	[*Enter Nurse and Peter.*]

罗丝玛丽花连在一起,我也不懂,反正你听了一定喜欢的。

罗密欧　替我向你小姐致意。

乳　母　一定一定。(罗密欧下)彼得!

彼　得　有!

乳　母　给我带路,拿着我的扇子,快些走。(同下)

第五场　同前。凯普莱特家的花园

(朱丽叶上)

朱丽叶　我在九点钟差奶妈去;她答应在半小时以内回来。也许她碰不见他;那是不会的。啊!她的脚走起路来不大方便。恋爱的使者应当是思想,因为它比驱散山坡上的阴影的太阳光还要快十倍;所以维纳斯的云车是用白鸽驾驶的,所以凌风而飞的丘比特生着翅膀。现在太阳已经升上中天,从九点钟到十二点钟是三个很长的钟点,可是她还没有回来。要是她是个有感情、有温暖的青春的血液的人,她的行动一定会像球儿一样敏捷,我用一句话就可以把她抛到我的心爱的情人那里,他也可以用一句话把她抛回到我这里;可是年纪老的人,大多像死人一般,手脚滞钝,呼唤不灵,慢腾腾地没有一点精神。

(乳母及彼得上)

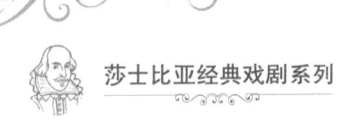

	O God, she comes! O honey nurse, what news?
	Hast thou met with him? Send thy man away.
Nurse	Peter, stay at the gate.
	[*Exit Peter.*]
JULIET	Now, good sweet nurse — O Lord, why look'st Thou sad?
	Though news be sad, yet tell them merrily;
	If good, thou shamest the music of sweet news
	By playing it to me with so sour a face.
Nurse	I am aweary, give me leave a while.
	Fie, how my bones ache! What a jaunce have I had!
JULIET	I would thou hadst my bones, and I thy news.
	Nay, come, I pray thee speak. Good, good nure, speak.
Nurse	Jesu, what haste! Can you not stay awhile?
	Do you not see that I am out of breath?
JULIET	How art thou out of breath when thou hast breath
	To say to me that thou art out of breath?
	The excuse that thou dost make in this delay
	Is longer than the tale thou dost excuse.
	Is thy news good or bad? Answer to that.
	Say either, and I'll stay the circumstance.
	Let me be satisfied, is't good or bad?
Nurse	Well, you have made a simple choice; you know not how to choose a man. Romeo? No, not he. Though his face be better than any man's, yet his leg excels all men's; and for a hand and a foot, and a body, though they be not to be talk'd on, yet they are past compare. He is not the flower of courtesy, but, I'll warrant him, as gentle as a lamb. Go thy ways, wench; serve God.

		啊,上帝!她来了。啊,好心肝奶妈!什么消息?你碰到他了吗?叫那个人出去。
乳	母	彼得,到门口去等着。(彼得下)
朱丽叶		亲爱的好奶妈——哎呀!你怎么满脸的懊恼?即使是坏消息,你也应该装着笑容说;如果是好消息,你就不该用这副难看的面孔奏出美妙的音乐来。
乳	母	我累死了,让我歇一会儿吧。哎呀,我的骨头好痛!我赶了多少的路!
朱丽叶		我但愿把我的骨头给你,你的消息给我。求求你,快说呀;好奶妈,说呀。
乳	母	耶稣哪!你忙什么?你不能等一下子吗?你没见我气都喘不过来吗?
朱丽叶		你既然气都喘不过来,那么你怎么会告诉我说你气都喘不过来?你费了这么久的时间推三阻四的,要是干脆告诉了我,还不是几句话就完了。我只要你回答我,你的消息是好的还是坏的?只要先回答我一个字,详细的话慢慢再说好了。快让我知道了吧,是好消息还是坏消息?
乳	母	好,你是个傻孩子,选中了这么一个人;你不知道怎样选一个男人。罗密欧!不,他不行,虽然他的脸长得比人家漂亮一点;可是他的腿才长得有样子;讲到他的手、他的脚、他的身体,虽然这种话不大好出口,可是的确谁也比不上他。他不顶懂得礼貌,可是温柔得就像一头羔羊。好,看你的运气吧,姑娘;好好敬

	What, have you din'd at home?
JULIET	No, no. But all this did I know before.
	What says he of our marriage? What of that?
Nurse	Lord, how my head aches! What a head have I!
	It beats as it would fall in twenty pieces.
	My back o' t' other side, — ah, my back, my back!
	Beshrew your heart for sending me about
	To catch my death with jauncing up and down!
JULIET	I' faith, I am sorry that thou art not well.
	Sweet, sweet, sweet nurse, tell me, what says my love?
Nurse	Your love says, like an honest gentleman, and a
	courteous, and a kind, and a handsome, and, I warrant,
	a virtuous — Where is your mother?
JULIET	Where is my mother? Why, she is within.
	Where should she be? How oddly thou repliest!
	'Your love says, like an honest gentleman,
	Where is your mother?'
Nurse	O God's Lady dear!
	Are you so hot? Marry come up, I trow.
	Is this the poultice for my aching bones?
	Henceforward do your messages yourself.
JULIET	Here's such a coil! Come, what says Romeo?
Nurse	Have you got leave to go to shrift to-day?
JULIET	I have.
Nurse	Then hie you hence to Friar Laurence' cell;
	There stays a husband to make you a wife.
	Now comes the wanton blood up in your cheeks;
	They'll be in scarlet straight at any news.
	Hie you to church; I must another way,

奉上帝。怎么，你在家里吃过饭了吗？

朱丽叶　没有，没有。你这些话我都早就知道了。他对于结婚的事情怎么说？

乳　母　主啊！我的头痛死了！我害了多厉害的头痛！痛得好像要裂成二十块似的。还有我那一边的背痛；哎哟，我的背！我的背！你的心肠真好，叫我到外边东奔西走去寻死。

朱丽叶　害你这样不舒服，我真是说不出的抱歉。亲爱的，亲爱的，亲爱的奶妈，告诉我，我的爱人说些什么话？

乳　母　你的爱人说——他说得很像个老老实实的绅士，很有礼貌，很和气，很漂亮，而且也很规矩——你的妈呢？

朱丽叶　我的妈！她就在里面；她还会在什么地方？你回答得多么古怪："你的爱人说，他说得很像个老老实实的绅士，你的妈呢？"

乳　母　哎哟，圣母娘娘！你这样性急吗？哼！反了反了，这就是你瞧着我筋骨酸痛而替我涂上的药膏吗？以后还是你自己去送信吧。

朱丽叶　别缠下去啦！快些，罗密欧怎么说？

乳　母　你已经得到准许今天去忏悔吗？

朱丽叶　我已经得到了。

乳　母　那么你快到劳伦斯神父的寺院里去，有一个丈夫在那边等着你去做他的妻子哩。现在你的脸红起来啦。你到教堂里去吧，我还要到别处去搬一张梯子来，等到

	To fetch a ladder, by the which your love
	Must climb a bird's nest soon when it is dark.
	I am the drudge, and toil in your delight;
	But you shall bear the burden soon at night.
	Go; I'll to dinner; hie you to the cell.
JULIET	Hie to high fortune! Honest nurse, farewell.
	〔*Exeunt.*〕

SCENE VI   The same. Friar Laurence's cell.

〔*Enter Friar Laurence and Romeo.*〕

Friar   So smile the heavens upon this holy act
That after-hours with sorrow chide us not!

ROMEO   Amen, amen! But come what sorrow can,
It cannot countervail the exchange of joy
That one short minute gives me in her sight.
Do thou but close our hands with holy words,
Then love-devouring death do what he dare—
It is enough I may but call her mine.

Friar   These violent delights have violent ends
And in their triumph die, like fire and powder,
Which, as they kiss, consume. The sweetest honey
Is loathsome in his own deliciousness
And in the taste confounds the appetite.
Therefore love moderately: long love doth so;
Too swift arrives as tardy as too slow.
〔*Enter Juliet.*〕
Here comes the lady. O, so light a foot
Will ne'er wear out the everlasting flint.

天黑的时候，你的爱人就可以凭着它爬进鸟巢里。为了使你快乐我就吃苦奔跑；可是你到了晚上也要负起那个重担来啦。去吧，我还没有吃过饭呢。

朱丽叶　我要找寻我的幸运去！好奶妈，再会。（各下）

第六场　同前。劳伦斯神父的寺院

（劳伦斯神父及罗密欧上）

劳伦斯　愿上天祝福这神圣的结合，不要让日后的懊恨把我们谴责！

罗密欧　阿门，阿门！可是无论将来会发生什么悲哀的后果，都抵不过我在看见她这短短一分钟内的欢乐。不管侵蚀爱情的死亡怎样伸展它的魔手，只要你用神圣的言语，把我们的灵魂结为一体，让我能够称她一声我的人，我也就不再有什么遗恨了。

劳伦斯　这种狂暴的快乐将会产生狂暴的结局，正像火和火药的亲吻，就在最得意的一刹那烟消云散。最甜的蜜糖可以使味觉麻木；不太热烈的爱情才会维持久远；太快和太慢，结果都不会圆满。

（朱丽叶上）

这位小姐来了。啊！这样轻盈的脚步，是永远不会踩

	A lover may bestride the gossamer
	That idles in the wanton summer air,
	And yet not fall; so light is vanity.
JULIET	Good even to my ghostly confessor.
Friar	Romeo shall thank thee, daughter, for us both.
JULIET	As much to him, else is his thanks too much.
ROMEO	Ah, Juliet, if the measure of thy joy
	Be heap'd like mine, and that thy skill be more
	To blazon it, then sweeten with thy breath
	This neighbour air, and let rich music's tongue
	Unfold the imagin'd happiness that both
	Receive in either by this dear encounter.
JULIET	Conceit, more rich in matter than in words,
	Brags of his substance, not of ornament.
	They are but beggars that can count their worth;
	But my true love is grown to such excess
	I cannot sum up sum of half my wealth.
Friar	Come, come with me, and we will make short work;
	For, by your leaves, you shall not stay alone
	Till Holy Church incorporate two in one.
	[*Exeunt.*]

破神龛前的砖石的；一个恋爱中的人，可以踏在随风飘荡的蛛网上而不会跌下，幻妄的幸福使他灵魂飘然轻举。

朱丽叶　晚安，神父。

劳伦斯　孩子，罗密欧会替我们两人感谢你的。

朱丽叶　我也向他同样问了好，他何必再来多余的客套。

罗密欧　啊，朱丽叶！要是你感觉到像我一样多的快乐，要是你的灵唇慧舌，能够宣述你衷心的快乐，那么让空气中满布着从你嘴里吐出来的芳香，用无比的妙乐把这一次会晤中我们两人给予彼此的无限欢欣倾吐出来吧。

朱丽叶　充实的思想不在于言语的富丽；只有乞儿才能够计数他的家私。真诚的爱情充溢在我的心里，我无法估计自己享有的财富。

劳伦斯　来，跟我来，我们要把这件事情早点办好；因为在神圣的教会没有把你们两人结合以前，你们两人是不能在一起的。（同下）

Act III

SCENE I *Verona. A public place.*

[*Enter Mercutio, Benvolio, and Men.*]

BENVOLIO I pray thee, good Mercutio, let's retire.
The day is hot, the Capulet abroad.
And if we meet, we shall not' scape a brawl,
For now, these hot days, is the mad blood stirring.

MERCUTIO Thou art like one of these fellows that, when he enters the confines of a tavern, claps me his sword upon the table and says 'God send me no need of thee!' and by the operation of the second cup draws him on the drawer, when indeed there is no need.

BENVOLIO Am I like such a fellow?

MERCUTIO Come, come, thou art as hot a Jack in thy mood as any in Italy; and as soon moved to be moody, and as soon moody to be moved.

BENVOLIO And what to?

MERCUTIO Nay, an there were two such, we should have none shortly, for one would kill the other. Thou! why, thou wilt quarrel with a man that hath a hair more or a hair less in his beard than thou hast. Thou wilt quarrel with a man for cracking nuts, having no other reason but because thou hast hazel eyes. What eye but such an eye would spy out such a quarrel? Thy head is as full of quarrels as an egg is full of meat; and yet thy head hath been beaten as addle as an egg for quarrelling.

第三幕

第一场 维罗纳。广场

（茂丘西奥、班伏里奥、侍童及若干仆人上）

班伏里奥　好茂丘西奥，咱们还是回去吧。天这么热，凯普莱特家里的人满街都是，要是碰到了他们，又免不了吵架；因为在这种热天气里，一个人的脾气最容易暴躁起来。

茂丘西奥　你就像这么一种家伙，跑进了酒店的门，把剑在桌子上一放，说，"上帝保佑我不要用到你！"等到两杯喝罢，却无缘无故拿起剑来跟酒保吵架。

班伏里奥　我难道是这样一种人吗？

茂丘西奥　得啦得啦，你的坏脾气比得上意大利无论哪一个人；动不动就要生气，一生气就要乱动。

班伏里奥　再以后怎样呢？

茂丘西奥　哼！要是有两个像你这样的人碰在一起，结果总会一个也没有，因为大家都要把对方杀死了方肯罢休。你！嘿，你会因为人家比你多一根或是少一根胡须，就跟人家吵架。瞧见人家剥栗子，你也会跟他闹翻，你的理由只是因为你有一双栗色的眼睛。除了生着这样一双眼睛的人以外，谁还会像这样吹毛求疵地去跟人家寻事？你的脑袋里装满了惹事招非的念头，正像鸡蛋里装满了蛋黄蛋白，虽然为了惹事招非的缘故，你的

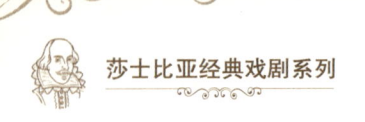

Thou hast quarrell'd with a man for coughing in the street, because he hath wakened thy dog that hath lain asleep in the sun. Didst thou not fall out with a tailor for wearing his new doublet before Easter, with another for tying his new shoes with an old riband? And yet thou wilt tutor me from quarrelling!

BENVOLIO An I were so apt to quarrel as thou art, any man should buy the feesimple of my life for an hour and a quarter.

MERCUTIO The feesimple? O simple!

[*Enter Tybalt and others.*]

BENVOLIO By my head, here come the Capulets.

MERCUTIO By my heel, I care not.

TYBALT Follow me close, for I will speak to them.
Gentlemen, good den. A word with one of you.

MERCUTIO And but one word with one of us?
Couple it with something; make it a word and a blow.

TYBALT You shall find me apt enough to that, sir, an you will give me occasion.

MERCUTIO Could you not take some occasion without giving?

TYBALT Mercutio, thou consortest with Romeo.

MERCUTIO Consort? What, dost thou make us minstrels? An thou make minstrels of us, look to hear nothing but discords. Here's my fiddlestick; here's that shall make you dance. Zounds, consort!

BENVOLIO We talk here in the public haunt of men.
Either withdraw unto some private place
And reason coldly of your grievances,

脑袋曾经给人打得像个坏蛋一样。你曾经为了有人在街上咳了一声嗽而跟他吵架，因为他咳醒了你那条在太阳底下睡觉的狗。不是有一次你因为看见一个裁缝在复活节以前穿起他的新背心来，所以跟他大闹吗？不是还有一次因为他用旧带子系他的新鞋子，所以又跟他大闹吗？现在你却要教我不要跟人家吵架！

班伏里奥　要是我像你一样爱吵架，不消一时半刻，我的性命早就卖给人家了。

（提伯尔特及余人等上）

茂丘西奥　性命卖给人家！哼，算了吧！

班伏里奥　哎哟！凯普莱特家里的人来了。

茂丘西奥　哼！我不在乎。

提伯尔特　你们跟着我不要走开，等我去向他们说话。两位晚安！我要跟你们中间无论哪一位说句话儿。

茂丘西奥　您只要跟我们两人中间的一个人讲一句话吗？再来点儿别的吧。要是您愿意在一句话以外，再跟我们较量一两手，那我们倒愿意奉陪。

提伯尔特　只要您给我一个理由，您就会知道我也不是个怕事的人。

茂丘西奥　您不会自己想出一个什么理由来吗？

提伯尔特　茂丘西奥，你陪着罗密欧到处乱闯——

茂丘西奥　到处拉唱！怎么！你把我们当作一群沿街卖唱的人吗？你要是把我们当作沿街卖唱的人，那么我们倒要请你听一点儿不大好听的声音；这就是我的提琴上的拉弓，拉一拉就要叫你跳起舞来。他妈的！到处拉唱！

班伏里奥　这儿来往的人太多，讲话不大方便，最好还是找个清静一点的地方去谈谈；要不然大家别闹意气，有什

	Or else depart. Here all eyes gaze on us.
MERCUTIO	Men's eyes were made to look, and let them gaze.
	I will not budge for no man's pleasure, I.
	[*Enter Romeo.*]
TYBALT	Well, peace be with you, sir. Here comes my man.
MERCUTIO	But I'll be hang'd, sir, if he wear your livery.
	Marry, go before to field, he'll be your follower!
	Your worship in that sense may call him man.
TYBALT	Romeo, the love I bear thee can afford
	No better term than this: thou art a villain.
ROMEO	Tybalt, the reason that I have to love thee
	Doth much excuse the appertaining rage
	To such a greeting. Vilain am I none.
	Therefore farewell. I see thou knowest me not.
TYBALT	Boy, this shall not excuse the injuries
	That thou hast done me; therefore turn and draw.
ROMEO	I do protest I never injur'd thee,
	But love thee better than thou canst devise
	Till thou shalt know the reason of my love;
	And so good Capulet, which name I tender
	As dearly as mine own, be satisfied.
MERCUTIO	O calm, dishonourable, vile submission!
	Alla stoccata carries it away. [*Draws.*]
	Tybalt, you ratcatcher,will you walk?
TYBALT	What wouldst thou have with me?
MERCUTIO	Good king of Cats, nothing but one of your nine lives.
	That I mean to make bold withal, and, as you shall use
	me hereafter, dry-beat the rest of the eight. Will you
	pluck your sword out of his pilcher by the ears? Make

过不去的事平心静气理论理论；否则各走各的路，也就完了，别让这么许多人的眼睛瞧着我们。

茂丘西奥 人们生着眼睛总要瞧，让他们瞧去好了；我可不能为着别人高兴离开这块地方。

（罗密欧上）

提伯尔特 好，我的人来了；我不跟你吵。

茂丘西奥 他又不吃你的饭，不穿你的衣，怎么是你的人？可是他虽然不是你的跟班，要是你拔脚逃起来，他倒一定会紧紧跟住你的。

提伯尔特 罗密欧，我对你的仇恨使我只能用一个名字称呼你——你是一个恶贼！

罗密欧 提伯尔特，我跟你无冤无恨，你这样无端挑衅，我本来是不能容忍的，可是因为我有必须爱你的理由，所以也不愿跟你计较了。我不是恶贼；再见，我看你还不知道我是个什么人。

提伯尔特 小子，你冒犯了我，现在可不能用这种花言巧语掩饰过去；赶快回过身子，拔出剑来吧。

罗密欧 我可以郑重声明，我从来没有冒犯过你，而且你想不到我是怎样爱你，除非你知道了我所以爱你的理由。所以，好凯普莱特——我尊重这一个姓氏，就像尊重我自己的姓氏一样——咱们还是讲和了吧。

茂丘西奥 哼，好丢脸的屈服！只有武力才可以洗去这种耻辱。（拔剑）提伯尔特，你这捉耗子的猫儿，你愿意跟我决斗吗？

提伯尔特 你要我跟你干么？

茂丘西奥 好猫精，听说你有九条性命，我只要取你一条命，留下那另外八条，等以后再跟你算账。快快拔出你的剑来，

	haste, lest mine be about your ears ere it be out.
TYBALT	I am for you. [*Daws.*]
ROMEO	Gentle Mercutio, put thy rapier up.
MERCUIIO	Come, sir, your passado!
	[*They fight.*]
ROMEO	Draw, Benvolio; beat down their weapons.
	Gentlemen, for shame! forbear this outrage!
	Tybalt, Mercutio, the Prince expressly hath
	Forbid this bandying in Verona streets.
	Hold, Tybalt! Good Mercutio!
	[*Tybalt under Romeo's arm thrusts Mercutio in, and flies with his Followers.*]
MERCUIIO	I am hurt.
	A plague o' both your houses! I am sped.
	Is he gone and hath nothing?
BENVOLIO	What, art thou hurt?
MERCUIIO	Ay, ay, a scratch, a scratch. Marry, 'tis enough.
	Where is my page? Go, villain, fetch a surgeon.
	[*Exit Page.*]
ROMEO	Courage, man. The hurt cannot be much.
MERCUTIO	No, 'tis not so deep as a well, nor so wide as a church door; but 'tis enough, 'twill serve. Ask for me tomorrow, and you shall find me a grave man. I am peppered, I warrant, for this world. A plague o' both your houses! Zounds, a dog, a rat, a mouse, a cat, to scratch a man to death! a braggart, a rogue, a villain, that fights by the book of arithmetic! Why the devil came you between us? I was hurt under your arm.
ROMEO	I thought all for the best.

罗密欧与朱丽叶
ROMEO AND JULIET

否则莫怪无情,我的剑就要临到你的耳朵边了。

提伯尔特	好,我愿意奉陪。(拔剑)
罗密欧	好茂丘西奥,收起你的剑。
茂丘西奥	来,来,来,我倒要领教领教你的剑法。(二人互斗)
罗密欧	班伏里奥,拔出剑来,把他们的武器打下来。两位老兄,这算什么?快别闹啦!提伯尔特,茂丘西奥,亲王已经明令禁止在维罗纳的街道上斗殴。住手,提伯尔特!好茂丘西奥!(提伯尔特及其党徒下)
茂丘西奥	我受伤了。你们这两家倒霉的人家!我已经完啦。他不带一点伤就去了吗?
班伏里奥	啊!你受伤了吗?
茂丘西奥	嗯,嗯,擦破了一点儿;可是也够受的了。我的侍童呢?你这家伙,快去找个外科医生来。(侍童下)
罗密欧	放心吧,老兄;这伤口不算十分厉害。
茂丘西奥	是的,它没有一口井那么深,也没有一扇门那么阔,可是这一点伤也就够要命的了;要是你明天找我,就到坟墓里来看我吧。我这一生是完了。你们这两家倒霉的人家!他妈的!狗、耗子、猫儿,都会咬得死人!这个说大话的家伙,这个混账东西,打起架来也要按照着数学的公式!谁叫你把身子插了进来?都是你把我拉住了,我才受了伤。
罗密欧	我完全是出于好意。

MERCUTIO	Help me into some house, Benvolio,
	Or I shall faint. A platue o' both your houses!
	They have made worms' meat of me. I have it,
	And soundly too. Your houses!
	[*Exit, supported by Benvolio.*]
ROMEO	This gentleman, the Prince's near ally,
	My very friend, hath got this mortal hurt
	In my behalf — my reputation stain'd
	With Tybalt's slander — Tybalt, that an hour
	Hath been my kinsman. O sweet Juliet,
	Thy beauty hath made me effeminate
	And in my temper soften'd valour's steel.
	[*Enter Benvolio.*]
BENVOLIO	O Romeo, Romeo, brave Mereutio's dead!
	That gallant spirit hath aspir'd the clouds,
	Which too untimely here did scorn the earth.
ROMEO	This day's black fate on moe days doth depend;
	This but begins the woe others must end.
	[*Enter Tybalt.*]
BENVOLIO	Here comes the furious Tybalt back again.
ROMEO	Alive in triumph, and Mercutio slain?
	Away to heaven respective lenity,
	And fire-ey'd fury be my conduct now!
	Now, Tybalt, take the 'villain' back again
	That late thou gavest me; for Mercutio's soul
	Is but a little way above our heads,
	Staying for thine to keep him company.
	Either thou or I, or both, must go with him.
TYBALT	Thou, wretched boy, that didst consort him here,

茂丘西奥 班伏里奥,快把我扶进什么屋子里去,不然我就要晕过去了。你们这两家倒霉的人家!我已经死在你们手里了。——你们这两家人家!(茂丘西奥,班伏里奥同下)

罗密欧 他是亲王的近亲,也是我的好友;如今他为了我的缘故受到了致命的重伤。提伯尔特杀死了我的朋友,又毁谤了我的名誉,虽然他在一小时以前还是我的亲人。亲爱的朱丽叶啊!你的美丽使我变得懦弱,磨钝了我的勇气的锋刃!

(班伏里奥重上)

班伏里奥 啊,罗密欧,罗密欧!勇敢的茂丘西奥死了;他已经撒手离开尘世,他的英魂已经升上天庭了!

罗密欧 今天这一场意外的变故,怕要引起日后的灾祸。

(提伯尔特重上)

班伏里奥 暴怒的提伯尔特又来了。

罗密欧 茂丘西奥死了,他却耀武扬威活在人世!现在我只好抛弃一切顾忌,不怕伤了亲戚的情分,让眼睛里喷出火焰的愤怒支配着我的行动了!提伯尔特,你刚才骂我恶贼,我要你把这两个字收回去;茂丘西奥的阴魂就在我们头上,他在等着你去跟他做伴;我们两个人中间必须有一个人去陪陪他,要不然就是两人一起死。

提伯尔特 你这该死的小子,你生前跟他做朋友,死后也去陪

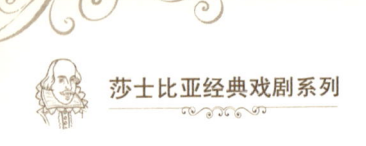

	Shalt with him hence.
ROMEO	This shall determine that.
	[*They fight. Tybalt falls.*]
BENVOLIO	Romeo, away, be gone!
	The citizens are up, and Tybalt slain.
	Stand not amaz'd. The Prince will doom thee death
	If thou art taken. Hence, be gone, away!
ROMEO	O, I am fortune's fool!
BENVOLIO	Why dost thou stay?
	[*Exit Romeo.*]
	[*Enter Citizens.*]
Citizen	Which way ran he that kill'd Mercutio?
	Tybalt, that murtherer, which way ran he?
BENVOLIO	There lies that Tybalt.
Citizen	Up, sir, go with me.
	I charge thee in the Prince's name obey.
	[*Enter Prince, attended, old Montague, Capulet, their wives, and others.*]
Prince	Where are the vile beginners of this fray?
BENVOLIO	O noble Prince. I can discover all
	The unlucky manage of this fatal brawl.
	There lies the man, slain by young Romeo,
	That slew thy kinsman, brave Mercutio.
Capulet's Wife	Tybalt, my cousin! O my brother's child!
	O Prince! O husband! O, the blood is spill'd
	Of my dear kinsman! Prince, as thou art true,
	For blood of ours shed blood of Montague.
	O cousin, cousin!
Prince	Benvolio, who began this bloody fray?

他吧!

罗密欧　这柄剑可以替我们决定谁死谁生。(二人互斗;提伯尔特倒下)

班伏里奥　罗密欧,快走!市民们都已经被这场争吵惊动了,提伯尔特又死在这儿。别站着发怔;要是你给他们捉住了,亲王就要判你死刑。快去吧!快去吧!

罗密欧　唉!我是受命运玩弄的人。

班伏里奥　你为什么还不走?(罗密欧下)

(市民等上)

市民甲　杀死茂丘西奥的那个人逃到哪儿去了?那凶手提伯尔特逃到什么地方去了?

班伏里奥　躺在那边的就是提伯尔特。

市民甲　先生,起来吧,请你跟我去。我用亲王的名义命令你服从。

(亲王率侍从;蒙太古夫妇、凯普莱特夫妇及余人等上)

亲王　这一场争吵的肇祸的罪魁在什么地方?

班伏里奥　啊,尊贵的亲王!我可以把这场流血的争吵的不幸的经过向您从头告禀。躺在那边的那个人,就是把您的亲戚,勇敢的茂丘西奥杀死的人,他现在已经被年轻的罗密欧杀死了。

凯普莱特夫人　提伯尔特,我的侄儿!啊,我的哥哥的孩子!亲王啊!侄儿啊!丈夫啊!哎哟!我的亲爱的侄儿给人杀死了!殿下,您是正直无私的,我们家里流的血,应当用蒙太古家里流的血来报偿。哎哟,侄儿啊!侄儿啊!

亲王　班伏里奥,是谁开始这场血斗的?

BENVOLIO	Tybalt, here slain, whom Romeo's hand did slay.
	Romeo, that spoke him fair, bid him bethink
	How nice the quarrel was, and urg'd withal
	Your high displeasure. All this — uttered
	With gentle breath, calm look, knees humbly bow'd —
	Could not take truce with the unruly spleen
	Of Tybalt deaf to peace, but that he tilts
	With piercing steel at bold Mercutio's breast;
	Who, all as hot, turns deadly point to point,
	And, with a martial scorn, with one hand beats
	Cold death aside and with the other sends
	It back to Tybalt, whose dexterity
	Retorts it. Romeo he cries aloud,
	'Hold, friends! friends part!' and swifter than his tongue,
	His agile arm beats down their fatal points,
	And 'twixt them rushes; underneath whose arm
	An envious thrust from Tybalt hit the life
	Of stout Mercutio, and then Tybalt fled;
	But by-and-by comes back to Romeo,
	Who had but newly entertain'd revenge,
	And to't they go like lightning; for, ere I
	Could draw to part them, was stout Tybalt shain;
	And, as he fell, did Romeo turn and fly.
	This is the truth, or let Benvolio die.
Capulet's Wife	He is a kinsman to the Montague;
	Affection makes him false, he speaks not true.
	Some twenty of them fought in this black strife,
	And all those twenty could but kill one life.
	I beg for justice, which thou, Prince, must give.

班伏里奥 死在这儿的提伯尔特,他是被罗密欧杀死的。罗密欧很诚恳地劝告他,叫他想一想这种争吵多么没意思,并且也提起您的森严的禁令。他用温和的语调、谦恭的态度,陪着笑脸向他反复劝解,可是提伯尔特充耳不闻,一味逞着他的骄横,拔出剑来就向勇敢的茂丘西奥胸前刺了过去;茂丘西奥也动了怒气,就和他两下交锋起来,自恃着本领高强,满不在乎地一手挡开了敌人致命的剑锋,一手向提伯尔特还刺过去,提伯尔特眼明手快,也把它挡开了。那个时候罗密欧就高声喊叫:"住手,朋友;两下分开!"说时迟,来时快,他的敏捷的腕臂已经打下了他们的利剑,他就插身在他们两人中间;谁料提伯尔特怀着毒心,冷不防打罗密欧的手臂下面刺了一剑过去,竟中了茂丘西奥的要害,于是他就逃走了。等了一会儿他又回来找罗密欧,罗密欧这时候正是满腔怒火,就像闪电似的跟他打起来,我还来不及拔剑阻止他们,勇猛的提伯尔特已经中剑而死,罗密欧见他倒在地上,也就转身逃走了。我所说的句句都是真话,倘有虚言,愿受死刑。

凯普莱特夫人 他是蒙太古家的亲戚,他说的话都是徇着私情,完全是假的。他们一共有二十来个人参加这场恶斗,二十个人合力谋害一个人的生命。殿下,我要请您主持公道,

	Romeo slew Tybalt; Romeo must not live.
Prince	Romeo slew him; he slew Mercutio.
	Who now the price of his dear blood doth owe?
MONTAGUE	Not Romeo, Prince; he was Mercutio's friend;
	His fault concludes but what the law should end,
	The life of Tybalt.
Prince	And for that offence
	Immediately we do exile him hence.
	I have an interest in your hate's proceeding,
	My blood for your rude brawls doth lie a-bleeding;
	But I'll amerce you with so strong a fine
	That you shall all repent the loss of mine.
	I will be deaf to pleading and excuses;
	Nor tears nor prayers shall purchase out abuses.
	Therefore use none. Let Romeo hence in haste,
	Else, when he is found, that hour is his last.
	Bear hence this body, and attend our will.
	Mercy but murders, pardoning those that kill.
	[*Exeunt.*]

SCENE II *The same. Capulet's orchard.*

[*Enter Juliet alone.*]

JULIET	Gallop apace, you fiery-footed steeds,
	Towards Phoebus' lodging! Such a wagoner
	As Phaeton would whip you to the West
	And bring in cloudy night immediately.
	Spread thy close curtain, love-performing night,
	That runaways' eyes may wink, and Romeo

罗密欧杀死了提伯尔特，罗密欧必须抵命。

亲　　　王　罗密欧杀了他，他杀了茂丘西奥；茂丘西奥的生命应当由谁抵偿？

蒙　太　古　殿下，罗密欧不应该偿他的命；他是茂丘西奥的朋友，他的过失不过是执行了提伯尔特依法应处的死刑。

亲　　　王　为了这一个过失，我现在宣布把他立刻放逐出境。你们双方的憎恨已经牵涉到我的身上，在你们残暴的斗殴中，已经流下了我的亲人的血；可是我要给你们一个重重的惩罚，警戒警戒你们的将来。我不要听任何的请求辩护，哭泣和祈祷都不能使我枉法徇情，所以不用想什么挽回的办法，赶快把罗密欧遣送出境吧；不然的话，我们什么时候发现他，就在什么时候把他处死。把这尸体抬去，不许违抗我的命令；对杀人的凶手不能讲慈悲，否则就是鼓励杀人了。（同下）

第二场　同前。凯普莱特家的花园

（朱丽叶上）

朱　丽　叶　快快跑过去吧，踏着火云的骏马，把太阳拖回到它的安息的所在；但愿驾车的法厄同鞭策你们飞驰到西方，让阴沉的暮夜赶快降临。展开你密密的帷幕吧，成全恋爱的黑夜！遮住夜行人的眼睛，让罗密欧悄悄地投

Leap to these arms untalk'd of and unseen.
Lovers can see to do their amorous rites
By their own beauties; or, if love be blind,
It best agrees with night. Come, civil night,
Thou sober-suited matron, all in black,
And learn me how to lose a winning match,
Play'd for a pair of stainless maidenhoods.
Hood my unmann'd blood, bating in my cheeks,
With thy black mantle till strange love, grown bold,
Think true love acted simple modesty.
Come, night; come, Romeo; come, thou day in night;
For thou wilt lie upon the wings of night
Whiter than new snow upon a raven's back.
Come, gentle night; come, loving, black-brow'd night;
Give me my Romeo; and, when he shall die,
Take him and cut him out in little stars,
And he will make the face of heaven so fine
That all the world will be in love with night
And pay no worship to the garish sun.
O, I have bought the mansion of a love,
But not possess'd it; and though I am sold,
Not yet enjoy'd. So tedious is this day
As is the night before some festival
To an impatient child that hath new robes
And may not wear them. O, here comes my nurse,
[*Enter nurse, with cords.*]
And she brings news; and every tongue that speaks
But Romeo's name speaks heavenly eloquence.
Now, nurse, what news? What hast thou there? the

入我的怀里,不被人家看见也不被人家谈论!恋人们可以在他们自身美貌的光辉里互相缱绻;即使恋爱是盲目的,那也正好和黑夜相称。来吧,温文的夜,你朴素的黑衣妇人,教会我怎样在一场全胜的赌博中失败,把各人纯洁的童贞互为赌注。用你黑色的罩巾遮住我脸上羞怯的红潮,等我深藏内心的爱情慢慢地胆大起来,不再因为在行动上流露真情而惭愧。来吧,黑夜!来吧,罗密欧!来吧,你黑夜中的白昼!因为你将要睡在黑夜的翼上,比乌鸦背上的新雪还要皎白。来吧,柔和的黑夜!来吧,可爱的黑颜的夜,把我的罗密欧给我!等他死了以后,你再把他带去,分散成无数的星星,把天空装饰得如此美丽,使全世界都恋爱着黑夜,不再崇拜炫目的太阳。啊!我已经买下了一所恋爱的华厦,可是它还不曾属我所有;虽然我已经把自己出卖,可是还没有被买主领去。这日子长得真叫人厌烦,正像一个做好了新衣服的小孩,在节日的前夜焦躁地等着天明一样。啊!我的奶妈来了。

(乳母携绳上)

她带着消息来了。谁的舌头上只要说出了罗密欧的名字,他就在吐露着天上的仙音。奶妈,什么消息?你

	cords
	That Romeo bid thee fetch?
Nurse	Ay, ay, the cords.
	[*Throws them down.*]
JULIET	Ay me! what news? Why dost thou wring thy hands?
Nurse	Ah, weraday! he's dead, he's dead, he's dead!
	We are undone, lady, we are undone!
	Alack the day! he's gone, he's kill'd, he's dead!
JULIET	Can heaven be so envious?
Nurse	Romeo can,
	Though heaven cannot. O Romeo, Romeo!
	Who ever would have thought it? Romeo!
JULIET	What devil art thou that dost torment me thus?
	This torture should be roar'd in dismal hell.
	Hath Romeo slain himself? Say thou but 'I',
	And that bare vowel 'I' shall poison more
	Than the death-darting eye of cockatrice.
	I am not I, if there be such an 'I';
	Or those eyes shut that makes thee answer 'I',
	If he be slain, say 'I'; or if not, 'no'.
	Brief sounds determine of my weal or woe.
Nurse	I saw the wound, I saw it with mine eyes,
	(God save the mark!) here on his manly breast.
	A piteous corse, a bloody piteous corse;
	Pale, pale as ashes, all bedaub'd in blood,
	All in gore-blood. I swounded at the sight.
JULIET	O, break, my heart! poor bankrout, break at once!
	To prison, eyes; ne'er look on liberty!
	Vile earth, to earth resign; end motion here,

		带着些什么来了？那就是罗密欧叫你去拿的绳子吗？
乳	母	是的，是的，这绳子。（将绳掷下）
朱丽叶		哎哟！什么事？你为什么扭着你的手？
乳	母	唉！唉！唉！他死了，他死了，他死了！我们完了，小姐，我们完了！唉！他去了，他给人杀了，他死了！
朱丽叶		天道竟会这样狠毒吗？
乳	母	不是天道狠毒，罗密欧才下得了这样狠毒的手。啊！罗密欧，罗密欧！谁想得到会有这样的事情？罗密欧！
朱丽叶		你是个什么鬼，这样煎熬着我？这简直就是地狱里的酷刑。罗密欧把他自己杀死了吗？你只要回答我一个"是"字，这一个"是"字就比毒龙眼里射放的死光更会致人死命。如果真有这样的事，我就不会再在人世，或者说，那叫你说声"是"的人，从此就要把眼睛紧闭。要是他死了，你就说"是"；要是他没有死，你就说"不"；这两个简单的字就可以决定我的终身祸福。
乳	母	我看见他的伤口，我亲眼看见他的伤口，慈悲的上帝！就在他的宽阔的胸上。一个可怜的尸体，一个可怜的流血的尸体，像灰一样苍白，满身都是血，满身都是一块块的血；我一瞧见就晕过去了。
朱丽叶		啊，我的心要碎了！——可怜的破产者，你已经丧失了一切，还是赶快碎裂了吧！失去了光明的眼睛，你从此不能再见天日了！你这俗恶的泥土之躯，赶快停

	And thou and Romeo press one heavy bier!
Nurse	O Tybalt, Tybalt, the best friend I had!
	O courteous Tybalt! honest gentleman,
	That ever I should live to see thee dead!
JULIET	What storm is this that blows so contrary?
	Is Romeo slaught'red, and is Tybalt dead?
	My dear-lov'd cousin, and my dearer lord?
	Then, dreadful trumpet, sound the general doom!
	For who is living, if those two are gone?
Nurse	Tybalt is gone, and Romeo banished;
	Romeo that kill'd him, he is banished.
JULIET	O, God! Did Romeo's hand shed Tybalt's blood?
Nurse	It did, it did! alas the day, it did!
JULIET	O serpent heart, hid with a flow'ring face!
	Did ever dragon keep so fair a cave?
	Beautiful tyrant! fiend angelical!
	Dove-feather'd raven! wolvish-ravening lamb!
	Despised substance of divinest show!
	Just opposite to what thou justly seem'st—
	A damned saint, an honourable villain!
	O nature, what hadst thou to do in hell
	When thou didst bower the spirit of a fiend
	In mortal paradise of such sweet flesh?
	Was ever book containing such vile matter
	So fairly bound? O, that deceit should dwell
	In such a gorgeous palace!
Nurse	There's no trust,
	No faith, no honesty in men; all perjur'd,
	All forsworn, an naught, all dissemblers.

　　　　　　止呼吸，复归于泥土，去和罗密欧同眠在一个圹穴里吧！

乳　　母　啊！提伯尔特，提伯尔特！我的顶好的朋友！啊，温文的提伯尔特，正直的绅士！想不到我活到今天，却会看见你死去！

朱丽叶　这是一阵什么风暴，一会儿又倒转方向！罗密欧给人杀了，提伯尔特又死了吗？一个是我的最亲爱的表哥，一个是我的更亲爱的夫君？那么，可怕的号角，宣布世界末日的来临吧！要是这样两个人都可以死去，谁还应该活在这世上？

乳　　母　提伯尔特死了，罗密欧放逐了；罗密欧杀了提伯尔特，他现在被放逐了。

朱丽叶　上帝啊！提伯尔特是死在罗密欧手里的吗？

乳　　母　是的，是的；唉！是的。

朱丽叶　啊，花一样的面庞里藏着蛇一样的心！那一条恶龙曾经栖息在这样清雅的洞府里？美丽的暴君！天使般的魔鬼！披着白鸽羽毛的乌鸦！豺狼一样残忍的羔羊！圣洁的外表包覆着丑恶的实质！你的内心刚巧和你的形状相反，一个万恶的圣人，一个庄严的奸徒！造物主啊！你为什么要从地狱里提出这一个恶魔的灵魂，把它安放在这样可爱的一座肉体的天堂里？哪一本邪恶的书籍曾经装订得这样美观？啊！谁想得到这样一座富丽的宫殿里，会容纳着欺人的虚伪！

乳　　母　男人都靠不住，没有良心，没有真心的；谁都是三心二意，反复无常，奸恶多端，尽是些骗子。啊！我的

	Ah, where's my man? Give me some aqua vitae.
	These griefs, these woes, these sorrows make me old.
	Shame come to Romeo!
JULIET	Blister'd be thy tongue
	For such a wish! He was not born to shame.
	Upon his brow shame is asham'd to sit;
	For 'tis a throne where honour may be crown'd
	Sole monarch of the universal earth.
	O, what a beast was I to chide at him!
Nurse	Will you speak well of him that kill'd your cousin?
JULIET	Shall I speak ill of him that is my husband?
	Ah, poor my lord, what tongue shall smooth thy name
	When I, thy three-hours wife, have mangled it?
	But wherefore, villain, didst thou kill my cousin?
	That villain cousin would have kill'd my husband.
	Back, foolish tears, back to your native spring!
	Your tributary drops belong to woe,
	Which you, mistaking, offer up to joy.
	My husband lives, that Tybalt would have slain;
	And Tybalt's dead, that would have slain my husband.
	All this is comfort; wherefore weep I then?
	Some word there was, worser than Tybalt's death,
	That murd'red me. I would forget it fain;
	But O, it presses to my memory
	Like damned guilty deeds to sinners' minds!
	'Tybalt is dead, and Romeo — banished.'
	That 'banished', that one word 'banished',
	Hath slain ten thousand Tybalts. Tybalt's death
	Was woe enough, if it had ended there;

人呢？快给我倒点儿酒来；这些悲伤烦恼，已经使我老起来了。愿耻辱降临到罗密欧的头上！

朱丽叶　你说出这样的愿望，你的舌头上就应该长起水疱来！耻辱从来不曾和他在一起，它不敢侵上他的眉宇，因为那是君临天下的荣誉的宝座。啊！我刚才把他这样辱骂，我真是个畜生！

乳　母　杀死了你的族兄的人，你还说他好话吗？

朱丽叶　他是我的丈夫，我应当说他坏话吗？啊！我的可怜的丈夫！你的三小时的妻子都这样凌辱你的名字，谁还会对它说一句温情的慰藉呢？可是你这恶人，你为什么杀死我的哥哥？他要是不杀死我的哥哥，我的凶恶的哥哥就会杀死我的丈夫。回去吧，愚蠢的眼泪，流回到你的源头；你那滴滴的细流，本来是悲哀的倾注，可是你却错把它呈献给喜悦。我的丈夫活着，他没有被提伯尔特杀死；提伯尔特死了，他想要杀死我的丈夫！这明明是喜讯，我为什么要哭泣呢？还有两个字比提伯尔特的死更使我痛心，像一柄利刃刺进了我的胸中；我但愿忘了它们，可是唉！它们紧紧地牢附在我的记忆里，就像萦回在罪人脑中的不可宥恕的罪恶。"提伯尔特死了，罗密欧放逐了！"放逐了！这"放逐"两个字，就等于杀死了一万个提伯尔特。单单提伯尔特的死，已经可以令人伤心了；即使祸不单行，必须

Or, if sour woe delights in fellowship
And needly will be rank'd with other griefs,
Why followed not, when she said 'Tybalt's dead,'
Thy father, or thy mother, nay, or both,
Which mordern lamentation might have mov'd?
But with a rear ward following Tybalt's death,
'Romeo is banished' —to speak that word
Is father, mother, Tybalt, Romeo, Juliet,
All slain, all dead. 'Romeo is banished'
There is no end, no limit,measure, bound,
In that word's death; no words can that woe sound.
Where is my father and my mother, nurse?

Nurse Weeping and wailing over Tybalt's corse.
Will you go to them? I will bring you thither.

JULIET Wash they his wounds with tears? Mine shall be spent,
When theirs are dry, for Romeo's banishment.
Take up those cords. Poor ropes, you are beguil'd,
Both you and I, for Romeo is exil'd.
He made yon for a highway to my bed;
But I, a maid, die maiden-widowed.
Come, cords; come, nurse. I'll to my wedding bed;
And death, not Romeo, take my maidenhead!

Nurse Hie to your chamber. I'll find Romeo
To comfort you. I wot well where he is.
Hark ye, your Romeo will be here at night.
I'll to him; he is hid at Laurence' cell.

JULIET O, find him! give this ring to my true knight
And bid him come to take his last farewell.

[*Exeunt.*]

在"提伯尔特死了"这一句话以后,再接上一句不幸的消息,为什么不说你的父亲,或是你的母亲,或是父母两人都死了,那也可以引起一点人情之常的哀悼?可是在提伯尔特的噩耗以后,再接连一记更大的打击,"罗密欧放逐了!"这句话简直等于说,父亲、母亲、提伯尔特、罗密欧、朱丽叶,一起被杀,一起死了。"罗密欧放逐了!"这一句话里面包含着无穷无际、无极无限的死亡,没有字句能够形容出这里面蕴蓄着的悲伤。——奶妈,我的父亲、我的母亲呢?

乳　母　他们正在抚着提伯尔特的尸体痛哭。你要去看他们吗?让我带着你去。

朱丽叶　让他们用眼泪洗涤他的伤口,我的眼泪是要留着为罗密欧的放逐而哀哭的。拾起那些绳子来。可怜的绳子,你是失望了,我们俩都失望了,因为罗密欧已经被放逐;他要借着你做接引相思的桥梁,可是我却要做一个独守空闺的怨女而死去。来,绳儿;来,奶妈。我要去睡上我的新床,把我的童贞奉献给死亡!

乳　母　那么你快到房里去吧;我去找罗密欧来安慰你,我知道他在什么地方。听着,你的罗密欧今天晚上一定会来看你;他现在躲在劳伦斯神父的寺院里,我就去找他。

朱丽叶　啊!你快去找他;把这指环拿去给我的忠心的骑士,叫他来做一次最后的诀别。(各下)

SCENE III The same. Friar Laurence's cell.

[Enter Friar Laurence.]

Friar Romeo, come forth; come forth, thou fearful man.
Affliction is enamour'd of thy parts,
And thou art wedded to calamity.

[Enter Romeo.]

ROMEO Father, what news? What is the Prince's doom
What sorrow craves acquaintance at my hand
That I yet know not?

Friar Too familiar
Is my dear son with such sour company.
I bring thee tidings of the Prince's doom.

ROMEO What less than doomsday is the Prince's doom?

Friar A gentler judgment vanish'd from his lips—
Not body's death, but body's banishment.

ROMEO Ha, banishment? Be merciful, say 'death';
For exile hath more terror in his look,
Much more than death. Do not say 'banishment'.

Friar Hence from Verona art thou banished.
Be patient, for the world is broad and wide.

ROMEO There is no world without Verona walls,
But purgatory, torture, hell itself.
Hence banished is banish'd from the world,
And world's exile is death. Then 'banishment'
Is death misterm'd. Calling death 'banishment',
Thou cut'st my head off with a golden axe
And smilest upon the stroke that murders me.

第三场　同前。劳伦斯神父的寺院

（劳伦斯神父上）

劳　伦　斯　罗密欧，跑出来；出来吧，你这受惊的人，你已经和坎坷的命运结下了不解之缘。

（罗密欧上）

罗　密　欧　神父，什么消息？亲王的判决怎样？还有什么我所不知道的不幸的事情将要来找我？

劳　伦　斯　我的好孩子，你已经遭逢到太多的不幸了。我来报告你亲王的判决。

罗　密　欧　除了死罪以外，还会有什么判决？

劳　伦　斯　他的判决是很温和的：他并不判你死罪，只宣布把你放逐。

罗　密　欧　嘿！放逐！慈悲一点，还是说"死"吧！不要说"放逐"，因为放逐比死还要可怕。

劳　伦　斯　你必须立刻离开维罗纳境内。不要懊恼，这是一个广大的世界。

罗　密　欧　在维罗纳城以外没有别的世界，只有地狱的苦难；所以从维罗纳放逐，就是从这世界上放逐，也就是死。明明是死，你却说是放逐，这就等于用一柄利斧砍下我的头，反因为自己犯了杀人罪而洋洋得意。

Friar　　　　O deadly sin! O rude unthankfulness!
　　　　　　　Thy fault our law calls death; but the kind Prince,
　　　　　　　Taking thy part, hath rush'd aside the law,
　　　　　　　And turn'd that black word death to banishment.
　　　　　　　This is dear mercy, and thou seest it not.

ROMEO　　'Tis torture, and not mercy. Heaven is here,
　　　　　　　Where Juliet lives; and every cat and dog
　　　　　　　And little mouse, every unworthy thing,
　　　　　　　Live here in heaven and may look on her;
　　　　　　　But Romeo may not. More validity,
　　　　　　　More honourable state, more courtship lives
　　　　　　　In carrion flies than Romeo. They may seize
　　　　　　　On the white wonder of dear Juliet's hand
　　　　　　　And steal immortal blessing from her lips,
　　　　　　　Who, even in pure and vestal modesty,
　　　　　　　Still blush, as thinking their own kisses sin;
　　　　　　　But Romeo may not, he is banished.
　　　　　　　This may flies do, when I from this must fly;
　　　　　　　They are free men, but I am banished.
　　　　　　　And sayest thou yet that exile is not death?
　　　　　　　Hadst thou no poison mix'd, no sharp-ground knife,
　　　　　　　No sudden mean of death, though ne'er so mean,
　　　　　　　But 'banished' to kill me —'banished'?
　　　　　　　O friar, the damned use that word in hell;
　　　　　　　Howling attends it! How hast thou the heart,
　　　　　　　Being a divine, a ghostly confessor,
　　　　　　　A sin-absolver, and my friend profess'd,
　　　　　　　To mangle me with that word 'banished'?

Friar　　　　Thou fond mad man, hear me a little speak.

劳伦斯 哎哟，罪过罪过！你怎么可以这样不知恩德！你所犯的过失，按照法律本来应该处死，幸亏亲王仁慈，特别对你开恩，才把可怕的死罪改成了放逐；这明明是莫大的恩典，你却不知道。

罗密欧 这是酷刑，不是恩典。朱丽叶所在的地方就是天堂；这儿的每一只猫、每一只狗、每一只小小的老鼠，都生活在天堂里，都可以瞻仰到她的容颜，可是罗密欧却看不见她。污秽的苍蝇都可以接触亲爱的朱丽叶的皎洁的玉手，从她的嘴唇上偷取天堂中的幸福，那两片嘴唇是这样的纯洁贞淑，永远含着娇羞，好像觉得它们自身的相吻也是一种罪恶；苍蝇可以这样做，我却必须远走高飞，它们是自由人，我却是一个放逐的流徒。你还说放逐不是死吗？难道你没有配好的毒药、锋锐的刀子或者无论什么致命的利器，而必须用"放逐"两个字把我杀害吗？放逐！啊，神父！只有沉沦在地狱里的鬼魂才会用到这两个字，伴着凄厉的呼号；你是一个教士，一个替人忏罪的神父，又是我的朋友，怎么忍心用"放逐"这两个字来寸磔我呢？

劳伦斯 你这痴心的疯子，听我说一句话。

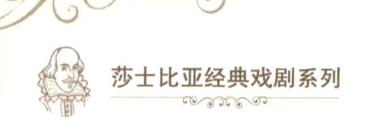

ROMEO	O, thou wilt speak again of banishment.
Friar	I'll give thee armour to keep off that word;
	Adversity's sweet milk, philosophy,
	To comfort thee, though thou art banished.
ROMEO	Yet 'banished'? Hang up philosophy!
	Unless philosophy can make a Juliet,
	Displant a town, reverse a prince's doom,
	It helps not, it prevails not. Talk no more.
Friar	O, then I see that madmen have no ears.
ROMEO	How should they, when that wise men have no eyes?
Friar	Let me dispute with thee of thy estate.
ROMEO	Thou canst not speak of that thou dost not feel.
	Wert thou as young as I, Juliet thy love,
	An hour but married, Tybalt murdered,
	Doting like me, and like me banished,
	Then mightst thou speak, then mightst thou tear thy hair,
	And fall upon the ground, as I do now,
	Taking the measure of an unmade grave.
	[*Knock within.*]
Friar	Arise; one knocks. Good Romeo, hide thyself.
ROMEO	Not I; unless the breath of heartsick groans,
	Mist-like infold me from the search of eyes. [*Knock.*]
Friar	Hark, how they knock! Who's there? Romeo, arise;
	Thou wilt be taken. — Stay awhile! —Stand up;
	[*Knock.*]
	Run to my study. — By-and-by! — God's will,
	What simpleness is this. — I come, I come!
	[*Knock.*]

罗密欧与朱丽叶
ROMEO AND JULIET

罗 密 欧　啊！你又要对我说起放逐了。

劳 伦 斯　我要教给你怎样抵御这两个字的方法，用哲学的甘乳安慰你的逆运，让你忘却被放逐的痛苦。

罗 密 欧　又是"放逐"！我不要听什么哲学！除非哲学能够制造一个朱丽叶，迁徙一个城市，撤销一个亲王的判决，否则它就没有什么用处。别再多说了吧。

劳 伦 斯　啊！那么我看疯人是不生耳朵的。

罗 密 欧　聪明人不生眼睛，疯人何必生耳朵呢？

劳 伦 斯　让我跟你讨论讨论你现在的处境吧。

罗 密 欧　你不能谈论你所没有感觉到的事情；要是你也像我一样年轻，朱丽叶是你的爱人，才结婚一小时，就把提伯尔特杀了；要是你也像我一样热恋，像我一样被放逐，那时你才可以讲话，那时你才会像我现在一样扯着你的头发，倒在地上，替自己量一个葬身的墓穴。（内叩门声）

劳 伦 斯　快起来，有人在敲门；好罗密欧，躲起来吧。

罗 密 欧　我不要躲，除非我心底里发出来的痛苦呻吟的气息，会像一重云雾一样把我掩过了追寻者的眼睛。（叩门声）

劳 伦 斯　听！门打得多么响！——是谁在外面？——罗密欧，快起来，你要给他们捉住了。——等一等！——站起来；（叩门声）跑到我的书斋里去。——就来了！——上帝啊！瞧你多么不听话！——来了，来了！（叩门

	Who knocks so hard? Whence come you? What's your will?
Nurse	[*Within.*] Let me come in, and you shall know my errand.
	I come from Lady Juliet.
Friar	Welcome then.
	[*Enter Nurse.*]
Nurse	O holy friar, O, tell me, holy friar
	Where is my lady's lord. where's Romeo?
Friar	There on the ground, with his own tears made drunk.
Nurse	O, he is even in my mistress' case,
	Just in her case!
Friar	O woeful sympathy!
	Piteous predicament!
Nurse	Even so lies she,
	Blubb'ring and weeping, weeping and blubbering.
	Stand up, stand up! Stand, an you be a man.
	For Juliet's sake, for her sake, rise and stand!
	Why should you fall into so deep an O?
ROMEO	[*Rises.*] Nurse —
Nurse	Ah sir! ah sir! Well, death's the end of all.
ROMEO	Spakest thou of Juliet? How is it with her?
	Doth not she think me an old murtherer,
	Now I have stain'd the childhood of our joy
	With blood remov'd but little from her own?
	Where is she? and how doth she! and what says
	My conceal'd lady to our cancell'd love?
Nurse	O, she says nothing, sir, but weeps and weeps;
	And now falls on her bed, and then starts up,

罗密欧与朱丽叶
ROMEO AND JULIET

声）谁把门敲得这么响？你是什么地方来的？你有什么事？

乳　　母　（在内）让我进来，你就可以知道我的来意；我是从朱丽叶小姐那里来的。

劳 伦 斯　那好极了，欢迎欢迎！

　　　　　（乳母上）

乳　　母　啊，神父！啊，告诉我，神父，我的小姐的姑爷呢？罗密欧呢？

劳 伦 斯　在那边地上哭得死去活来的就是他。

乳　　母　啊！他正像我的小姐一样，正像她一样！

劳 伦 斯　唉！真是同病相怜，一般的伤心！

乳　　母　她也是这样躺在地上，一边唠叨一边哭，一边哭一边唠叨。起来，起来；是个男子汉就该起来；为了朱丽叶的缘故，为了她的缘故，站起来吧。为什么您要伤心到这个样子呢？

罗 密 欧　奶妈！

乳　　母　唉，姑爷！唉，姑爷！一个人到头来总是要死的。

罗 密 欧　你刚才不是说起朱丽叶吗？她现在怎么样？我现在已经用她近亲的血玷污了我们的新欢，她不会把我当作一个杀人的凶犯吗？她在什么地方？她怎么样？我这位秘密的新妇对于我们这一段中断的情缘说了些什么话？

乳　　母　啊，她没有说什么话，姑爷，只是哭呀哭的哭个不停；一会儿倒在床上，一会儿又跳了起来；一会儿叫一声

	And Tybalt calls; and then on Romeo cries,
	And then down falls again.
ROMEO	As if that name,
	Shot from the deadly level of a gun,
	Did murther her; as that name's cursed hand
	Murder'd her kinsman. O, tell me, friar, tell me,
	In what vile part of this anatomy
	Doth my name lodge? Tell me, that I may sack
	The hateful mansion. [*Draws his dagger.*]
Friar	Hold thy desperate hand.
	Art thou a man? Thy form cries ont thou art;
	Thy tears are womanish, thy wild acts denote
	The unreasonable fury of a beast.
	Unseemly woman in a seeming man!
	Or ill-beseeming beast in seeing both!
	Thou hast amaz'd me. By my holy order,
	I thought thy dispositon better temper'd.
	Hast thou slain Tybalt? Wilt thou slay thyself?
	And slay thy lady that in thy life lives,
	By doing damned hate upon thyself?
	Why railest thou on thy birth, the heaven, and earth?
	Since birth and heaven and earth, all three do meet
	In thee at once; which thou at once wouldst lose.
	Fie, fie, thou shamest thy shape, thy love, thy wit,
	Which, like a usurer, abound'st in all,
	And usest none in that true use indeed
	Which should bedeck thy shape, thy love, thy wit.
	Thy noble shape is but a form of wax
	Digressing from the valour of a man;

罗密欧与朱丽叶
ROMEO AND JULIET

提伯尔特，一会儿哭一声罗密欧；然后又倒了下去。

罗密欧　好像我那一个名字是从枪口里瞄准了射出来似的，一弹出去就把她杀死，正像我这一双该死的手杀死了她的亲人一样。啊！告诉我，神父，告诉我，我的名字是在我身上哪一处万恶的地方？告诉我，好让我捣毁这可恨的巢穴。（拔剑）

劳伦斯　放下你的卤莽的手！你是一个男子吗？你的形状是一个男子，你却流着妇人的眼泪；你的狂暴的举动，简直是一头野兽的无可理喻的咆哮。你这须眉的贱妇，你这人头的畜类！我真想不到你的性情竟会这样毫无涵养。你已经杀死了提伯尔特，你还要杀死你自己吗？你没想到你对自己采取了这种万劫不赦的暴行就是杀死与你相依为命的你的妻子吗？为什么你要怨恨天地，怨恨你自己的生不逢辰？天地好容易生下你这一个人来，你却要亲手把你自己摧毁！呸！呸！你有的是一副堂堂的七尺之躯，有的是热情和智慧，你却不知道把它们好好利用，这岂不是辜负了你的七尺之躯，辜负了你的热情和智慧？你的堂堂的仪表不过是一尊蜡像，没有一点男子汉的血气；你的山盟海誓都是些空虚的谎语，杀害你所发誓珍爱的情人；你的智慧不知道指示你的行动，驾御你的感情，它已经变成了愚妄的谬见，正像装在一个笨拙的兵士的枪膛里的火药，本来是自卫的武器，因为不懂得点燃的方法，反而毁损了自己的肢体。怎么！起来吧，孩子！你刚才几乎

Thy dear love sworn but hollow perjury,
Killing that love which thou hast vow'd to cherish;
Thy wit, that ornament to shape and love,
Misshapen in the conduct of them both,
Like powder in a skilless soldier's flask,
Is set afire by thine own ignorance,
And thou dismemb'red with thine own defence.
What, rouse thee, man! Thy Juliet is alive,
For whose dear sake thou wast but lately dead.
There art thou happy. Tybalt would kill thee,
But thou slewest Tybalt. There art thou happy too.
The law, that threat'ned death, becomes thy friend
And turns it to exile. There art thou happy.
A pack of blessings light upon thy back;
Happiness courts thee in her best array;
But, like a misbehav'd and sullen wench,
Thou pout'st upon thy fortune and thy love.
Take heed, take heed, for such die miserable.
Go get thee to thy love, as was decreed,
Ascend her chamber, hence and comfort her.
But look thou stay not till the watch be set,
For then thou canst not pass to Mantua,
Where thou shalt live till we can find a time
To blaze your marriage, reconcile your friends,
Beg pardon of the Prince, and call thee back
With twenty hundred thousand times more joy
Than thou went'st forth in lamentation.
Go before, nurse. Commend me to thy lady,
And bid her hasten all the house to bed,

要为了你的朱丽叶而自杀,可是她现在好好活着,这是你的第一件幸事。提伯尔特要把你杀死,可是你却杀死了提伯尔特,这是你的第二件幸事。法律上本来规定杀人抵命,可是它对你特别留情,减成了放逐的处分,这是你的第三件幸事。这许多幸事照顾着你,幸福穿着盛装向你献媚,你却像一个倔强乖僻的女孩,向你的命运和爱情噘起了嘴唇。留心,留心,像这样不知足的人是不得好死的。去,快去会见你的情人,按照预定的计划,到她的寝室里去,安慰安慰她;可是在逻骑没有出发以前,你必须及早离开,否则你就到不了曼图亚。你可以暂时在曼图亚住下,等我们觑着机会,把你们的婚姻宣布出来,和解了你们两家的亲族,向亲王请求特赦,那时我们就可以用超过你现在离别的悲痛二百万倍的欢乐招呼你回来。奶妈,你先去,替我向你家小姐致意;叫她设法催促她家里的人早早安睡,他们在遭到这样重大的悲伤以后,这是

	Which heavy sorrow makes them apt unto.

                  Romeo is coming.

Nurse   O Lord, I could have stay'd here all the night
To hear good counsel. O, what learning is!
My lord, I'll tell my lady you will come.

ROMEO   Do so, and bid my sweet prepare to chide.

Nurse   Here is a ring she bid me give you, sir.
Hie you, make haste, for it grows very late.
[*Exit.*]

ROMEO   How well my comfort is reviv'd by this!

Friar   Go hence; good night; and here stands all your state:
Either be gone before the watch be set,
Or by the break of day disguis'd from hence.
Sojourn in Mantua. I'll find out your man,
And he shall signify from time to time
Every good hap to you that chances here.
Give me thy hand. 'Tis late. Farewell; goodnight.

ROMEO   But that a joy past joy calls out on me,
It were a grief so brief to part with thee.
Farewell.
[*Exeunt.*]

SCENE IV   *The same. Capulet's house.*

[*Enter old Capulet, his wife, and Paris.*]

CAPULET   Things have fall'n out, sir, so unluckily
That we have had no time to move our daughter.
Look you, she lov'd her kinsman Tybalt dearly,
And so did I. Well, we were born to die.

	很容易办到的。你对她说,罗密欧就要来了。
乳　　母	主啊！像这样好的教训,我就是在这儿听上一整夜都愿意；啊！真是有学问人说的话！姑爷,我就去对小姐说您就要来了。
罗 密 欧	很好,请你再叫我的爱人预备好一顿责骂。
乳　　母	姑爷,这一个戒指小姐叫我拿来送给您,请您赶快就去,天色已经很晚了。(下)
罗 密 欧	现在我又重新得到了多大的安慰！
劳 伦 斯	去吧,晚安！你的命运在此一举：你必须在巡逻者没有开始查缉以前脱身,否则就得在黎明时候化装逃走。你就在曼图亚安下身来；我可以找到你的仆人,倘使这儿有什么关于你的好消息,我会叫他随时通知你。把你的手给我。时候不早了,再会吧。
罗 密 欧	倘不是一个超乎一切喜悦的喜悦在招呼着我,像这样匆匆的离别,一定会使我黯然神伤。再会！(各下)

第四场　同前。凯普莱特家中一室

(凯普莱特、凯普莱特夫人及帕里斯上)

凯 普 莱 特	伯爵,舍间因为遭逢变故,我们还没有时间去开导小女；您知道她跟她那个表兄提伯尔特是友爱很笃的,我也非常喜欢他；唉！人生不免一死,也不必再去说他了。

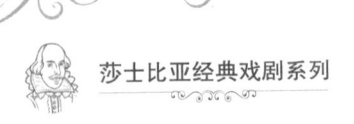

	'Tis very late; she'll not come down to-night.
	I promise you, but for your company,
	I would have been abed an hour ago.
PARIS	These times of woe afford no times to woo.
	Madam, goodnight. Commend me to your daughter.
Lady	I will, and know her mind early to-morrow;
	To-night she's mew'd up to her heaviness.
CAPULET	Sir Paris, I will make a desperate tender
	Of my child's love. I think she will be rul'd
	In all respects by me; nay more, I doubt it not.
	Wife, go you to her ere you go to bed;
	Acquaint her here of my son Paris' love
	And bid her (mark you me?) on Wednesday next —
	But, soft! what day is this?
PARIS	Monday, my lord.
CAPULET	Monday! ha, ha! Well, Wednesday is too soon.
	Thursday let it be — a Thursday, tell her
	She shall be married to this noble earl.
	Will you be ready? Do you like this haste?
	We'll keep no great ado — a friend or two;
	For hark you, Tybalt being slain so late,
	It may be thought we held him carelessly,
	Being our kinsman, if we revel much.
	Therefore we'll have some half a dozen friends,
	And there an end. But what say you to Thursday?
PARIS	My lord, I would that Thursday were to-morrow.
CAPULET	Well, get you gone. A Thursday be it then.
	Go you to Juliet ere you go to bed;
	Prepare her, wife, against this wedding day.

现在时间已经很晚，她今夜不会再下来了；不瞒您说，倘不是您大驾光临，我也早在一小时以前上了床啦。

帕 里 斯　我在你们正在伤心的时候来此求婚，实在是太冒昧了。晚安，伯母；请您替我向令爱致意。

凯普莱特夫人　好，我明天一早就去探听她的意思；今夜她已经怀着满腔的悲哀关上门睡了。

凯 普 莱 特　帕里斯伯爵，我可以大胆替我的孩子做主，我想她一定会绝对服从我的意志；是的，我对于这一点可以断定。夫人，你在临睡以前先去看看她，把这位帕里斯伯爵向她求爱的意思告诉她知道；你再对她说，听好我的话，叫她在星期三——且慢！今天星期几？

帕 里 斯　星期一，老伯。

凯 普 莱 特　星期一！哈哈！好，星期三是太快了点儿，那么就是星期四吧。对她说，在这个星期四，她就要嫁给这位尊贵的伯爵。您来得及准备吗？您不嫌太匆促吗？咱们也不必十分铺张，略为请几位亲友就够了；因为提伯尔特才死不久，他是我们自己家里的人，要是我们大开欢宴，人家也许会说我们对去世的人太没有情分。所以我们只要请五、六个亲友，把仪式举行一下就算了。您说星期四怎样？

帕 里 斯　老伯，我但愿星期四便是明天。

凯 普 莱 特　好，你去吧；那么就是星期四。夫人，你在临睡前先去看看朱丽叶，叫她预备预备，好做起新娘来啊。再见，

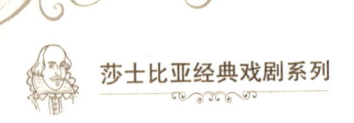

Farewell, My lord. — Light to my chamber, ho!
Afore me, It is so very very late
That we may call it early by-and-by.
Good night.

[*Exeunt.*]

SCENE V   *The same. Juliet's chamber*

[*Enter Romeo and Juliet aloft, at the Window.*]

JULIET   Wilt thou be gone? It is not yet near day.
It was the nightingale, and not the lark,
That pierc'd the fearful hollow of thine ear.
Nightly she sings on yond pomegranate tree.
Believe me, love, it was the nightingale.

ROMEO   It was the lark, the herald of the morn;
No nightingale. Look, love, what envious streaks
Do lace the severing clouds in yonder East.
Night's candles are burnt out, and jocund day
Stands tiptoe on the misty mountain tops.
I must be gone and live, or stay and die.

JULIET   Yond light is not daylight; I know it, I.
It is some meteor that the sun exhales
To be to thee this night a torchbearer
And light thee on the way to Mantua.
Therefore stay yet; thou need'st not to be gone.

ROMEO   Let me be ta'en, let me be put to death.
I am content, so thou wilt have it so.
I'll say yon grey is not the morning's eye,
'Tis but the pale reflex of Cynthia's brow;

伯爵。喂！掌灯！时候已经很晚了，等一会儿我们就要说时间很早了。晚安！（各下）

第五场　同前。朱丽叶的卧室

（罗密欧及朱丽叶上）

朱丽叶　你现在就要走了吗？天亮还有一会儿呢。那刺进你惊恐的耳膜中的，不是云雀，是夜莺的声音；它每天晚上在那边石榴树上歌唱。相信我，爱人，那是夜莺的歌声。

罗密欧　那是报晓的云雀，不是夜莺。瞧，爱人，不作美的晨曦已经在东天的云朵上镶起了金线，夜晚的星光已经烧尽，愉快的白昼蹑足踏上了迷雾的山巅。我必须到别处去找寻生路，或者留在这儿束手等死。

朱丽叶　那光明不是晨曦，我知道；那是从太阳中吐射出来的流星，要在今夜替你拿着火炬，照亮你到曼图亚去。所以你不必急着要去，再耽搁一会儿吧。

罗密欧　让我被他们捉住，让我被他们处死；只要是你的意思，我就毫无怨恨。我愿意说那边灰白色的云彩不是黎明睁开它的睡眼，那不过是从月亮的眉宇间反映出来的微光；那响彻云霄的歌声，也不是出于云雀的喉中。

	Nor that is not the lark whose notes do beat
	The vaulty heaven so high above our heads.
	I have more care to stay than will to go.
	Come, death, and welcome! Juliet wills it so.
	How is't, my soul? Let's talk; it is not day.
JULIET	It is, it is! Hie hence, be gone, away!
	It is the lark that sings so out of tune,
	Straining harsh discords and unpleasing sharps.
	Some say the lark makes sweet division;
	This doth not so, for she divideth us.
	Some say the lark and loathed toad chang'd eyes;
	O, now I would they had chang'd voices too,
	Since arm from arm that voice doth us affray,
	Hunting thee hence with hunt's-up to the day!
	O, now be gone! More light and light it grows.
ROMEO	Move light and light — more dark and dark our woes!
	[Enter Nurse.]
Nurse	Madam!
JULIET	Nurse?
Nurse	Your lady mother is coming to your chamber.
	The day is broke; be wary, look about.
	[Exit.]
JULIET	Then, window, let day in, and let life out.
ROMEO	Farewell, farewell! One kiss, and I'll descend.
	[He goeth down.]
JULIET	Art thou gone so, my lord, my love, my friend?
	I must hear from thee every day in the hour,
	For in a minute there are many days.
	O, by this count I shall be much in years

我巴不得留在这里,永远不要离开。来吧,死,我欢迎你!因为这是朱丽叶的意思。怎么,我的灵魂?让我们谈谈;天还没有亮哩。

朱丽叶　天已经亮了,天已经亮了;快走吧,快走吧!那唱得这样刺耳、嘶着粗涩的噪声和讨厌的锐音的,正是天际的云雀。有人说云雀会发出千变万化的甜蜜的歌声,这句话一点不对,因为它只使我们彼此分离;有人说云雀曾经和丑恶的蟾蜍交换眼睛,啊!我但愿它们也交换了声音,因为那声音使你离开了我的怀抱,用催醒的晨歌催促你登程。啊!现在你快走吧;天越来越亮了。

罗密欧　天越来越亮,我们悲哀的心却越来越黑暗。

　　　　（乳母上）

乳　　母　小姐!

朱丽叶　奶妈?

乳　　母　你的母亲就要到你房里来了。天已经亮啦,小心点儿。

　　　　（下）

朱丽叶　那么窗啊,让白昼进来,让生命出去。

罗密欧　再会,再会!给我一个吻,我就下去。

　　　　（由窗口下降）

朱丽叶　你就这样走了吗?我的夫君,我的爱人,我的朋友!我必须在每一小时内的每一天听到你的消息,因为一分钟就等于许多天。啊!照这样计算起来,等我再看

	Ere I again behold my Romeo!
ROMEO	Farewell!
	I will omit no opportunity
	That may convey my greetings, love, to thee.
JULIET	O, think'st thou we shall ever meet again?
ROMEO	I doubt it not; and all these woes shall serve
	For sweet discourses in our time to come.
JULIET	O God, I have an ill-divining soul!
	Methinks I see thee, now thou art below,
	As one dead in the bottom of a tomb.
	Either my eyesight fails, or thou look'st pale.
ROMEO	And trust me, love, in my eye so do you.
	Dry sorrow drinks our blood. Adieu, adieu!
	[*Exit.*]
JULETO	O Fortune, Fortune! all men call thee fickle.
	If thou art fickle, what dost thou with him
	That is renown'd for faith? Be fickle, Fortune,
	For then I hope thou wilt not keep him long
	But send him back.
Lady	[*Within.*] Ho, daughter! are you up?
JULIET	Who is't that calls? It is my lady mother.
	Is she not down so late, or up so early?
	What unaccustom'd cause procures her hither?
	Enter Mother.
Lady	Why, how now, Juliet?
JULIET	Madam, I am not well.
Lady	Evermore weeping for your cousin's death?
	What, wilt thou wash him from his grave with tears?
	An if thou couldst, thou couldst not make him live.

罗密欧与朱丽叶
ROMEO AND JULIET

见我的罗密欧的时候,我不知道已经老到怎样了。

罗密欧 再会!我决不放弃任何的机会,爱人,向你传达我的衷忱。

朱丽叶 啊!你想我们会不会再有见面的日子?

罗密欧 一定会有的;我们现在这一切悲哀痛苦,到将来便是握手谈心的资料。

朱丽叶 上帝啊!我有一颗预感不祥的灵魂;你现在站在下面,我仿佛望见你像一具坟墓底下的尸骸。也许是我的眼光昏花,否则就是你的面容太惨白了。

罗密欧 相信我,爱人,在我的眼中你也是这样;忧伤吸干了我们的血液。再会!再会!(下)

朱丽叶 命运啊命运!谁都说你反复无常;要是你真的反复无常,那么你怎样对待一个忠贞不贰的人呢?愿你不要改变你的轻浮的天性,因为这样也许你会早早打发他回来。

凯普莱特夫人 (在内)喂,女儿!你起来了吗?

朱丽叶 谁在叫我?是我的母亲吗?——难道她这么晚还没有睡觉,还是这么早就起来了?什么特殊的原因使她到这儿来?

(凯普莱特夫人上)

凯普莱特夫人 啊!怎么,朱丽叶!

朱丽叶 母亲,我不大舒服。

凯普莱特夫人 老是为了你表兄的死而掉泪吗?什么!你想用眼泪把他从坟墓里冲出来吗?就是冲得出来,你也没法子叫他复活;所以还是算了吧。适当的悲哀可以表示感情

	Therefore have done. Some grief shows much of love;
	But much of grief shows still some want of wit.
JULIET	Yet let me weep for such a feeling loss.
Lady	So shall you feel the loss, but not the friend
	Which you weep for.
JULIET	Feeling so the loss,
	I cannot choose but ever weep the friend.
Lady	Well, girl, thou weep'st not so much for his death
	As that the villain lives which slaughter'd him.
JULIET	What villain, madam?
Lady	That same villain Romeo,
JULIET	[*Aside.*] Villain and he be many miles asunder. —
	God pardon him! I do, with all my heart;
	And yet no man like he doth grieve my heart.
Lady	That is because the traitor murderer lives.
JULIET	Ay, madam, from the reach of these my hands.
	Would none but I might venge my cousin's death!
Lady	We will have vengeance for it, fear thou not.
	Then weep no more. I'll send to one in Mantua,
	Where that same banish'd runagate doth live,
	Shall give him such an unaccustom'd dram
	That he shall soon keep Tybalt company;
	And then I hope thou wilt be satisfied.
JULIET	Indeed I never shall be satisfied
	With Romeo till I behold him — dead —
	Is my poor heart so for a kinsman vex'd.
	Madam, if you could find out but a man
	To bear a poison, I would temper it;
	That Romeo should, upon receipt thereof,

朱　丽　叶	的深切，过度的伤心却可以证明智慧的欠缺。
朱　丽　叶	可是让我为了这样一个痛心的损失而流泪吧。
凯普莱特夫人	损失固然痛心，可是一个失去的亲人，不是眼泪哭得回来的。
朱　丽　叶	因为这损失实在太痛心了，我不能不为了失去的亲人而痛哭。
凯普莱特夫人	好，孩子，人已经死了，你也不用多哭他了；顶可恨的是那杀死他的恶人仍旧活在世上。
朱　丽　叶	什么恶人，母亲？
凯普莱特夫人	就是罗密欧那个恶人。
朱　丽　叶	（旁白）恶人跟他相去真有十万八千里呢。——上帝饶恕他！我愿意全心饶恕他；可是没有一个人像他那样使我心里充满了悲伤。
凯普莱特夫人	那是因为这个万恶的凶手还活在世上。
朱　丽　叶	是的，母亲，我恨不得把他抓住在我的手里。但愿我能够独自报复这一段杀兄之仇！
凯普莱特夫人	我们一定要报仇的，你放心吧；别再哭了。这个亡命的流徒现在到曼图亚去了，我要差一个人到那边去，用一种希有的毒药把他毒死，让他早点儿跟提伯尔特见面；那时候我想你一定可以满足了。
朱　丽　叶	真的，我心里永远不会感到满足，除非我看见罗密欧在我的面前——死去；我这颗可怜的心是这样为了一个亲人而痛楚！母亲，要是您能够找到一个愿意带毒药去的人，让我亲手把它调好，好叫那罗密欧服下以后，

	Soon sleep in quiet. O, how my heart abhors
	To hear him nam'd and cannot come to him,
	To wreak the love I bore my cousin Tybalt
	Upon his body that hath slaughter'd him!
Lady	Find thou the means, and I'll find such a man.
	But now I'll tell thee joyful tidings, girl.
JULIET	And joy comes well in such a needy time.
	What are they, I beseech your ladyship?
Lady	Well, well, thou hast a careful father, child;
	One who, to put thee from thy heaviness,
	Hath sorted out a sudden day of joy
	That thou expects not nor I look'd not for.
JULIET	Madam, in happy time! What day is that?
Lady	Marry, my child, early next Thursday morn
	The gallant, young, and noble gentleman,
	The County Paris, at Saint Peter's Church,
	Shall happily make thee there a joyful bride.
JULIET	Now by Saint Peter's Church, and Peter too,
	He shall not make me there a joyful bride!
	I wonder at this haste, that I must wed
	Ere he that should be husband comes to woo.
	I pray you tell my lord and father, madam,
	I will not marry yet; and when I do, I swear
	It shall be Romeo, whom you know I hate,
	Rather than Paris. These are news indeed!
Lady	Here comes your father. Tell him so yourself,
	And see how he will take it at your hands.
	[*Enter Capulet and Nurse.*]
CAPULET	When the sun sets the air doth drizzle dew,

就会安然睡去。唉！我心里多么难过，只听到他的名字，却不能赶到他的面前，为了我对哥哥的感情，我巴不得能在那杀死他的人的身上报这个仇！

凯普莱特夫人 你去想办法，我一定可以找到这样一个人。可是，孩子，现在我要告诉你好消息。

朱丽叶 在这样不愉快的时候，好消息来得真是再适当没有了。请问母亲，是什么好消息呢？

凯普莱特夫人 哈哈，孩子，你有一个体贴你的好爸爸哩；他为了替你排解愁闷已经为你选定了一个大喜的日子，不但你想不到，就是我也没有想到。

朱丽叶 母亲，快告诉我，是什么日子？

凯普莱特夫人 哈哈，我的孩子，星期四的早晨，那位风流年少的贵人，帕里斯伯爵，就要在圣彼得教堂里娶你做他的幸福的新娘了。

朱丽叶 望着圣彼得教堂和圣彼得的名字起誓，我决不让他娶我做他的幸福的新娘。世间哪有这样匆促的事情，人家还没有来向我求过婚，我倒先做了他的妻子了！母亲，请您对我的父亲说，我现在还不愿意出嫁；就是要出嫁，我可以发誓，我也宁愿嫁给我所痛恨的罗密欧，不愿嫁给帕里斯。真是些好消息！

凯普莱特夫人 你爸爸来啦；你自己对他说去，看他会不会听你的话。

（凯普莱特及乳母上）

凯普莱特 太阳西下的时候，天空中落下了蒙蒙的细露；可是我

But for the sunset of my brother's son
It rains downright.
How now? a conduit, girl? What, still in tears?
Evermore show'ring? In one little body
Thou counterfeit'st a bark, a sea, a wind:
For still thy eyes, which I may call the sea,
Do ebb and flow with tears; the bark thy body is
Sailing in this salt flood; the winds, thy sighs,
Who, raging with thy tears and they with them,
Without a sudden calm will overset
Thy tempest-tossed body. How now, wife?
Have you delivered to her our decree?

Lady Ay, sir; but she will none, she gives you thanks.
I would the fool were married to her grave!

CAPULET Soft! take me with you, take me with you, wife.
How? Will she none? Doth she not give us thanks?
Is she not proud? Doth she not count her blest,
Unworthy as she is, that we have wrought
So worthy a gentleman to be her bridegroom?

JULIET Not proud you have, but thankful that you have.
Proud can I never be of what I hate,
But thankful even for hate that is meant love.

CAPULET How, how, how, how, choplogic? What is this?
'Proud'— and 'I thank you'— and 'I thank you not'—
And yet 'not proud'? Mistress minion you,
Thank me no thankings, nor proud me no prouds,
But fettle your fine joints 'gainst Thursday next
To go with Paris to Saint Peter's Church,
Or I will drag thee on a hurdle thither.

的侄儿死了，却有倾盆的大雨送着他下葬。怎么！装起喷水管来了吗，孩子？咦！还在哭吗？雨到现在还没有停吗？你这小小的身体里面，也有船，也有海，也有风；因为你的眼睛就是海，永远有泪潮在那儿涨退；你的身体是一艘船，在这泪海上面航行；你的叹息是海上的狂风；你的身体经不起风浪的吹打，会在这汹涌的怒海中覆没的。怎么，妻子！你没有把我们的主意告诉她吗？

凯普莱特夫人 我告诉她了；可是她说谢谢你，她不要嫁人。我希望这傻丫头还是死了干净！

凯普莱特 且慢！讲明白点儿，讲明白点儿，妻子。怎么！她不要嫁人吗？她不谢谢我们吗？她不称心吗？像她这样一个贱丫头，我们替她找到了这么一位高贵的绅士做她的新郎，她还不想想这是多大的福气吗？

朱丽叶 我没有喜欢，只有感激；你们不能勉强我喜欢一个我对他没有好感的人，可是我感激你们爱我的一片好心。

凯普莱特 怎么！怎么！胡说八道！这是什么话？什么"喜欢""不喜欢"，"感激""不感激"！好丫头，我也不要你感谢，我也不要你喜欢，只要你预备好星期四到圣彼得教堂里去跟帕里斯结婚；你要是不愿意，我就把你装在木

	Out, you green-sickness carrion! out, you baggage!
	You tallow-face!
Lady	Fie, fie! what, are you mad?
JULIET	Good father, I beseech you on my knees,
	Hear me with patience but to speak a word.
CAPULET	Hang thee, young baggage! disobedient wretch!
	I tell thee what — get thee to church a Thursday
	Or never after look me in the face.
	Speak not, reply not, do not answer me!
	My fingers itch. Wife, we scarce thought us blest
	That God had lent us but this only child;
	But now I see this one is one too much,
	And that we have a curse in having her.
	Out on her, hilding!
Nurse	God in heaven bless her!
	You are to blame, my lord, to rate her so.
CAPULET	And why, my Lady Wisdom? Hold your tongue,
	Good Prudence. Smatter with your gossips, go!
Nurse	I speak no treason.
CAPULET	O, God-i-god-en!
Nurse	May not one speak?
CAPULET	Peace, you mumbling fool!
	Utter your gravity o'er a gossip's bowl,
	For here we need it not.
Lady	You are too hot.
CAPULET	God's bread! it makes me mad.
	Day, night, late, early,
	At home, abroad, alone, in company,
	Walking or sleeping, still my care hath been

	笼里拖了去。不要脸的死丫头，贱东西！
凯普莱特夫人	哎哟！哎哟！你疯了吗？
朱　丽　叶	好爸爸，我跪下来求求您，请您耐心听我说一句话。
凯 普 莱 特	该死的小贱妇！不孝的畜生！我告诉你，星期四给我到教堂里去，不然以后再也不要见我的面。不许说话，不要回答我；我的手指痒着呢。——夫人，我们常常怨叹自己福薄，只生下这一个孩子；可是现在我才知道就是这一个已经太多了，总是家门不幸，出了这一个冤孽！不要脸的贱货！
乳　　　母	上帝祝福她！老爷，您不该这样骂她。
凯 普 莱 特	为什么不该！我的聪明的老太太？谁要你多嘴，我的好大娘？你去跟你那些婆婆妈妈们谈天去吧，去！
乳　　　母	我又没有说过一句冒犯您的话。
凯 普 莱 特	啊，去你的吧。
乳　　　母	人家就不能开口吗？
凯 普 莱 特	闭嘴，你这叽里咕噜的蠢婆娘！我们不要听你的教训。
凯普莱特夫人	你的脾气太躁了。
凯 普 莱 特	哼！我气都气疯啦。每天每夜，时时刻刻，不论忙着空着，独自一个人或是跟别人在一起，我心里总是在

	To have her match'd; and having now provided
	A gentleman of princely parentage,
	Of fair demesnes, youthful, and nobly train'd,
	Stuff'd, as they say, with honourable parts,
	Proportion'd as one's thought would wish a man —
	And then to have a wretched puling fool,
	A whining mammet, in her fortune's tender,
	To answer 'I'll not wed, I cannot love;
	I am too young, I pray you pandon me'!
	But, an you will not wed, I'll pardon you.
	Graze where you will, you shall not house with me.
	Look to't, think on't; I do not use to jest.
	Thursday is near; lay hand on heart, advise:
	An you be mine, I'll give you to my friend;
	An you be not, hang, beg, starve, die in the streets,
	For, by my soul, I'll ne'er aeknowledge thee,
	Nor what is mine shall never do thee good.
	Trust to't. Bethink you. I'll not he forsworn.
	[*Exit.*]
JULIET	Is there no pity sitting in the clouds
	That sees into the bottom of my grief?
	O sweet my mother, cast me not away!
	Delay this marriage for a month, a week;
	Or if you do not, make the bridal bed
	In that dim monument where Tybalt lies.
Lady	Talk not to me , for I'll not speak a word.
	Do as thou wilt, for I have done with thee.
	[*Exit.*]
JULIET	O God!— O nurse, how shall this be prevented?

罗密欧与朱丽叶
ROMEO AND JULIET

盘算着怎样把她许配给一份好好的人家；现在好容易找到一位出身高贵的绅士，又有家私，又年轻，又受过高尚的教养，正是人家说的十二分的人才，好到没得说的了；偏偏这个不懂事的傻丫头，放着送上门来的好福气不要，说什么"我不要结婚""我不懂恋爱""我年纪太小""请你原谅我"；好，你要是不愿意嫁人，我可以放你自由，尽你的意思到什么地方去，我这屋子里可容不得你了。你给我想想明白，我是一向说到哪里做到哪里的。星期四就在眼前；自己仔细考虑考虑。你倘然是我的女儿，就得听我的话嫁给我的朋友；你倘然不是我的女儿，那么你去上吊也好，做叫花子也好，挨饿也好，死在街道上也好，我都不管，因为凭着我的灵魂发誓，我是再也不会认你这个女儿的，你也别想我会分一点什么给你。我不会骗你，你想一想吧；我已经发过誓了，我一定要把它做到。（下）

朱　丽　叶　天知道我心里是多么难过，难道它竟会不给我一点慈悲吗？啊，我的亲爱的母亲！不要丢弃我！把这门亲事延期一个月或是一个星期也好；或者要是您不答应我，那么请您把我的新床安放在提伯尔特长眠的幽暗的坟茔里吧！

凯普莱特夫人　不要对我讲话，我没有什么话好说的。随你的便吧，我是不管你啦。（下）

朱　丽　叶　上帝啊！啊，奶妈！这件事情怎么避过去呢？我的丈

	My husband is on earth, my faith in heaven.
	How shall that faith return again to earth
	Unless that husband send it me from heaven
	By leaving earth? Comfort me, counsel me.
	Alack, alack, that heaven should practise stratagems
	Upon so soft a subject as myself!
	What say'st thou? Hast thou not a word of joy?
	Some comfort, nurse.
Nurse	Faith, here it is.
	Romeo is banish'd; and all the world to nothing
	That he dares ne'er come back to challenge you;
	Or if he do, it needs must be by stealth.
	Then, since the case so stands as now it doth,
	I think it best you married with the County.
	O, he's a lovely gentleman!
	Romeo's a dishclout to him. An eagle, madam,
	Hath not so green, so quick, so fair an eye
	As Paris hath. Beshrew my very heart,
	I think you are happy in this second match,
	For it excels your first; or if it did not,
	Your first is dead — or 'twere as good he were
	As living here and you no use of him.
JULIET	Speak'st thou this from thy heart?
Nurse	And from my soul too; else beshrew them both.
JULIET	Amen!
Nurse	What?
JULIET	Well, thou hast comforted me marvellous much.
	Go in; and tell my lady I am gone,
	Having displeas'd my father, to Laurence' cell,

夫还在世间，我的誓言已经上达天听；倘使我的誓言可以收回，那么除非我的丈夫已经脱离人世，从天上把它送还给我。安慰安慰我，替我想想办法吧。唉！唉！想不到天也会捉弄像我这样一个柔弱的人！你怎么说？难道你没有一句可以使我快乐的话吗？奶妈，给我一点安慰吧！

乳　　母　好，那么你听我说。罗密欧是已经被放逐了；我可以拿随便什么东西跟你打赌，他再也不敢回来责问你，除非他偷偷地溜了回来。事情既然这样，那么我想你最好还是跟那伯爵结婚吧。啊！他真是个可爱的绅士！罗密欧比起他来只好算是一块抹布；小姐，一只鹰也没有像帕里斯那样一双又是碧绿好看，又是锐利的眼睛。说句该死的话，我想你这第二个丈夫，比第一个丈夫好得多啦；纵然不是好得多，可是你的第一个丈夫虽然还在世上，对你已经没有什么用处，也就跟死了差不多啦。

朱丽叶　你这些话是从心里说出来的吗？

乳　　母　那不但是我心里的话，也是我灵魂里的话；倘有虚假，让我的灵魂下地狱。

朱丽叶　阿门！

乳　　母　什么！

朱丽叶　好，你已经给了我很大的安慰。你进去吧；告诉我母亲说我出去了，因为得罪了我的父亲，要到劳伦斯

	To make confession and to be absolv'd.
Nurse	Marry, I will; and this is wisely done.
	[*Exit.*]
JULIET	Ancient damnation! O most wicked fiend!
	Is it more sin to wish me thus forsworn,
	Or to dispraise my lord with that same tongue
	Which she hath prais'd him with above compare
	So many thousand times? Go, counsellor!
	Thou and my bosom henceforth shall be twain.
	I'll to the friar to know his remedy.
	If all else fail, myself have power to die.
	[*Exit.*]

的寺院里去忏悔我的罪过。

乳　　母　很好，我就这样告诉她；这才是聪明的办法哩。（下）

朱　丽　叶　老而不死的魔鬼！顶丑恶的妖精！她希望我背弃我的盟誓；她几千次向我夸奖我的丈夫，说他比谁都好，现在却又用同一条舌头说他的坏话！去，我的顾问；从此以后，我再也不把你当作心腹看待了。我要到神父那儿去向他求救；要是一切办法都已用尽，我还有死这条路。（下）

Act IV

SCENE I *Verona. Friar Laurence's cell.*

[*Enter Friar Laurence and County Paris.*]

Friar On Thursday, sir? The time is very short.
PARIS My father Capulet will have it so,
And I am nothing slow to slack his haste.
Friar You say you do not know the lady's mind.
Uneven is the course; I like it not.
PARIS Immoderately she weeps for Tybalt's death,
And therefore have I little talk'd of love;
For Venus smiles not in a house of tears.
Now, sir, her father counts it dangerous
That she do give her sorrow so much sway,
And in his wisdom hastes our marriage
To stop the inundation of her tears,
Which, too much minded by herself alone,
May be put from her by society.
Now do you know the reason of this haste.
Friar [*Aside.*] I would I knew not why it should be slow'd.—
Look, sir, here comes the lady toward my cell.
[*Enter Juliet.*]
PARIS Happily met, my lady and my wife!
JULIET That may be, sir, when I may be a wife.
PARIS That may be must be, love, on Thursday next.
JULIET What must be shall be.
Friar That's a certain text.
PARIS Come you to make confession to this father?

第四幕

第一场 维罗纳。劳伦斯神父的寺院

（劳伦斯神父及帕里斯上）

劳 伦 斯　在星期四吗，伯爵？时间未免太局促了。

帕 里 斯　这是我的岳父凯普莱特的意思；他既然这样性急，我也不愿把时间延迟下去。

劳 伦 斯　您说您还没有知道那小姐的心思；我不赞成这种片面决定的事情。

帕 里 斯　提伯尔特死后她伤心过度，所以我没有跟她多谈恋爱，因为在一间哭哭啼啼的屋子里，维纳斯是露不出笑容来的。神父，她的父亲因为瞧她这样一味忧伤，恐怕会发生什么意外，所以才决定提早替我们完婚，免得她一天到晚哭得像个泪人儿一般；一个人在房间里最容易触景伤情，要是有了伴侣，也许可以替她排除悲哀。现在您可以知道我这次匆促结婚的理由了。

劳 伦 斯　（旁白）我希望我不知道它为什么必须延迟的理由。——瞧，伯爵，这位小姐到我寺里来了。

（朱丽叶上）

帕 里 斯　您来得正好，我的爱妻。

朱 丽 叶　伯爵，等我做了妻子以后，也许您可以这样叫我。

帕 里 斯　爱人，也许到星期四这就要成为事实了。

朱 丽 叶　事实是无可避免的。

劳 伦 斯　那是当然的道理。

帕 里 斯　您是来向这位神父忏悔的吗？

JULIET	To answer that, I should confess to you.
PARIS	Do not deny to him that you love me.
JULIET	I will confess to you that I love him.
PARIS	So will ye, I am sure, that you love me.
JULIET	If I do so, it will be of mere price,
	Being spoke behind your back, than to your face.
PARIS	Poor soul, thy face is much abus'd with tears.
JULIET	The tears have got small victory by that,
	For it was bad enough before their spite.
PARIS	Thou wrong'st it more than tears with that report.
JULIET	That is no slander, sir, which is a truth;
	And what I spake, I spake it to my face.
PARIS	Thy face is mine, and thou hast sland'red it.
JULIET	It may be so, for it is not mine own.
	Are you at leisure, holy father, now,
	Or shall I come to you at evening mass
Friar	My leisure serves me, pensive daughter, now.
	My lord, we must entreat the time alone.
PARIS	God shield I should disturb devotion!
	Juliet, on Thursday early will I rouse ye.
	Till then, adieu, and keep this holy kiss. [*Exit.*]
JULIET	O, shut the door! and when thou hast done so,
	Come weep with me — past hope, past cure, past help!
Friar	Ah, Juliet, I already know thy grief;
	It strains me past the compass of my wits.
	I hear thou must, and nothing may prorogue it,
	On Thursday next be married to this County.
JULIET	Tell me not, friar, that thou hear'st of this,
	Unless thou tell me how I may prevent it.

朱丽叶	回答您这一个问题,我必须向您忏悔了。
帕里斯	不要在他的面前否认您爱我。
朱丽叶	我愿意在您的面前承认我爱他。
帕里斯	我相信您也一定愿意在我的面前承认您爱我。
朱丽叶	要是我必须承认,那么在您的背后承认,比在您的面前承认好得多啦。
帕里斯	可怜的人儿!眼泪已经毁损了你的美貌。
朱丽叶	眼泪并没有得到多大的胜利;因为我这副容貌在没有被眼泪毁损以前,已经够丑了。
帕里斯	你不该说这样的话诽谤你的美貌。
朱丽叶	这不是诽谤,伯爵,这是实在的话,我当着我自己的脸说的。
帕里斯	你的脸是我的,你不该侮辱它。
朱丽叶	也许是的,因为它不是我自己的。神父,您现在有空吗?还是让我在晚祷的时候再来?
劳伦斯	我还是现在有空,多愁的女儿。伯爵,我们现在必须请您离开我们。
帕里斯	我不敢打扰你们的祈祷。朱丽叶,星期四一早我就来叫醒你;现在我们再会吧,请你保留下这一个神圣的吻。(下)
朱丽叶	啊!把门关了!关了门,再来陪着我哭吧。没有希望、没有补救、没有挽回了!
劳伦斯	啊,朱丽叶!我早已知道你的悲哀,实在想不出一个万全的计策。我听说你在星期四必须跟这伯爵结婚,而且毫无拖延的可能了。
朱丽叶	神父,不要对我说你已经听见这件事情,除非你能够

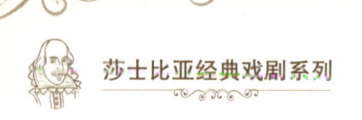

If in thy wisdom thou canst give no help,
Do thou but call my resolution wise
And with this knife I'll help it presently.
God join'd my heart and Romeo's, thou our hands;
And ere this hand, by thee to Romeo's seal'd,
Shall be the label to another deed,
Or my true heart with treacherous revolt
Turn to another, this shall slay them both.
Therefore, out of thy long-experienc'd time,
Give me some present counsel; or, behold,
'Twixt my extremes and me this bloody knife
Shall play the umpire, arbitrating that
Which the commission of thy years and art
Could to no issue of me honour bring.
Be not so long to speak. I long to die
If what thou speak'st speak not of remedy.

Friar Hold, daughter. I do spy a kind of hope,
Which craves as desperate an execution
As that is desperate which we would prevent.
If, rather than to marry County Paris
Thou hast the strength of will to slay thyself,
Then it is likely thou wilt undertake
A thing like death to chide away this shame,
That cop'st with death himself to scape from it;
And, if thou dar'st, I'll give thee remedy.

JULIET O, bid me leap, rather than marry Paris,
From off the battlements of any tower,
Or walk in thievish ways, or bid me lurk
Where sequents are; chain me with roaring bears,

告诉我怎样避免它;要是你的智慧不能帮助我,那么只要你赞同我的决心,我就可以立刻用这把刀解决一切。上帝把我的心和罗密欧的心结合在一起,我们两人的手是你替我们结合的;要是我这一只已经由你证明和罗密欧缔盟的手,再去和别人缔结新盟,或是我的忠贞的心起了叛变,投进别人的怀里,那么这把刀可以割下这背盟的手,诛戮这叛变的心。所以,神父,凭着你的丰富的见识阅历,请你赶快给我一些指教;否则瞧吧,这把血腥气的刀,就可以在我跟我的困难之间做一个公证人,替我解决你的经验和才能所不能替我觅得一个光荣解决的难题。不要老是不说话;要是你不能指教我一个补救的办法,那么我除了一死以外,没有别的希冀。

劳　伦　斯　住手,女儿;我已经望见了一线希望,可是那必须用一种非常的手段,方才能够抵御这一种非常的变故。要是你因为不愿跟帕里斯伯爵结婚,能够毅然立下视死如归的决心,那么你也一定愿意采取一种和死差不多的办法,来避免这种耻辱;倘然你敢冒险一试,我就可以把办法告诉你。

朱　丽　叶　啊!只要不嫁给帕里斯,你可以叫我从那边塔顶的雉堞上跳下来;你可以叫我在盗贼出没、毒蛇潜迹的路上匍匐行走;把我和咆哮的怒熊锁禁在一起;或者在夜间把我关在堆积尸骨的地窟里,用许多陈死的白骨、霉臭的腿胴和失去下颚的焦黄的骷髅掩盖着我的身体;

Or shut me nightly in a charnel house,
O'ercover'd quite with dead men's rattling bones,
With reeky shanks and yellow chapless skulls;
Or bid me go into a new-made grave
And hide me with a dead man in his shroud —
Things that, to hear them told, have made me tremble —
And I will do it without fear or doubt,
To live an unstain'd wife to my sweet love.

Friar   Hold, then. Go home, be merry, give consent
To marry Paris. Wednesday is to-morrow.
To-morrow night look that thou lie alone;
Let not the nurse lie with thee in thy chamber.
Take thou this vial, being then in bed,
And this distilled liquor drink thou off;
When presently through all thy veins shall run
A cold and drowsy humour; for no pulse
Shall keep his native progress, but surcease;
No warmth, no breath, shall testify thou livest;
The roses in thy lips and cheeks shall fade
To paly ashes, thy eyes' windows fall
Like death when he shuts up the day of life;
Each part, depriv'd of supple govermnent,
Shall, stiff and stark and cold, appear like death;
And in this borrowed likeness of shrunk death
Thou shalt continue two-and-forty hours,
And then awake as from a pleasant sleep.
Now, when the bridegroom in the morning comes
To rouse thee from thy bed, there art thou dead.
Then, as the manner of our country is,

或者叫我跑进一座新坟里去，把我隐匿在死人的殓衾里；无论什么使我听了战栗的事，只要可以让我活着对我的爱人做一个纯洁无瑕的妻子，我都愿意毫不恐惧、毫不迟疑地做去。

劳伦斯　好，那么放下你的刀，快快乐乐地回家去，答应嫁给帕里斯。明天就是星期三了；明天晚上你必须一人独睡，别让你的奶妈睡在你的房间里；这一个药瓶你拿去，等你上床以后，就把这里面炼就的液汁一口喝下，那时就会有一阵昏昏沉沉的寒气通过你全身的血管，接着脉搏就会停止跳动；没有一丝热气和呼吸可以证明你还活着；你的嘴唇和颊上的红色都会变成灰白；你的眼睑闭下，就像死神的手关闭了生命的白昼；你身上的每一部分失去了灵活的控制，都像死一样僵硬寒冷；在这种与死无异的状态中，你必须经过四十二小时，然后你就仿佛从一场酣睡中醒了过来。当那新郎在早晨来催你起身的时候，他们会发现你已经死了；然后，照着我们国里的规矩，他们就要给你穿起

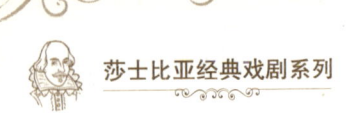

	In thy best robes uncovered on the bier
	Thou shalt be borne to that same ancient vault
	Where all the kindred of the Capulets lie.
	In the mean time, against thou shalt awake,
	Shall Romeo by my letters know our drift;
	And hither shall he come; and he and I
	Will watch thy waking, and that very night
	Shall Romeo bear thee hence to Mantua.
	And this shall free thee from this present shame,
	If no inconstant toy nor womanish fear
	Abate thy valour in the acting it.
JULIET	Give me, give me! O, tell not me of fear!
Friar	Hold! Get you gone, be strong and prosperous
	In this resolve. I'll send a friar with speed
	To Mantua, with my letters to thy lord.
JULIET	Love give me strength!and strength shall help afford.
	Farewell, dear father.
	[*Exeunt.*]

SCENE II　　*The same. Capulet's house.*

[*Enter Father Capulet, Mother, Nurse and Servingmen, two or three.*]

CAPULET　　So many guests invite as here are writ.
　　　　　　　[*Exit a Servingman.*]
　　　　　　　Sirrah, go hire me twenty cunning cooks.

Servant　　You shall have none ill, sir; for I'll try if they can lick their fingers.

CAPULET　　How canst thou try them so?

盛装，用柩车载着你到凯普莱特族中祖先的坟茔里。同时因为要预备你醒来，我可以写信给罗密欧，告诉他我们的计划，叫他立刻到这儿来；我跟他两个人就守在你的身边，等你一醒过来，当夜就叫罗密欧带着你到曼图亚去。只要你不临时变卦，不中途气馁，这一个办法一定可以使你避免这一场眼前的耻辱。

朱丽叶　给我！给我！啊，不要对我说起害怕两个字！

劳伦斯　拿着；你去吧，愿你意志坚强，前途顺利！我就叫一个弟兄飞快到曼图亚，带我的信去送给你的丈夫。

朱丽叶　爱情啊，给我力量吧！只有力量可以搭救我。再会，亲爱的神父！（各下）

第二场　同前。凯普莱特家中厅堂

（凯普莱特、凯普莱特夫人、乳母及众仆上）

凯普莱特　这单子上有名字的，都是要去邀请的客人。（仆甲下）来人，给我去雇二十个有本领的厨子来。

仆乙　老爷，您请放心，我一定要挑选能舔手指头的厨子来做菜。

凯普莱特　你怎么知道他们能做菜呢？

Servant	Marry, sir, 'tis an ill cook that cannot lick his own fingers. Therefore he that cannot lick his fingers goes not with me.
CAPULET	Go, begone. [*Exit Servingman.*] We shall be much unfurnish'd for this time. What, is my daughter gone to Friar Laurence?
Nurse	Ay, forsooth.
CAPULET	Well, he may chance to do some good on her. A peevish self-will'd harlotry it is. [*Enter Juliet.*]
Nurse	See where she comes from shrift with merry look.
CAPULET	How now, my headstrong? Where have you been gadding?
JULIET	Where I have learnt me to repent the sin Of disobedient opposition To you and your behests, and am enjoin'd By holy Laurence to fall prostrate here To beg your pardon. Pardon, I beseech you! Henceforward I am ever rul'd by you.
CAPULET	Send for the County. Go tell him of this. I'll have this knot knit up to-morrow morning.
JULIET	I met the youthful lord at Laurence' cell And gave him what becomed love I might, Not stepping o'er the bounds of modesty.
CAPULET	Why, I am glad on't. This is well. Stand up. This is as't should be. Let me see the County. Ay, marry, go, I say, and fetch him hither.

仆　　　乙　呀，老爷，不能舔手指头的就不能做菜；这样的厨子我就不要。

凯普莱特　好，去吧。咱们这一次实在有点儿措手不及。什么！我的女儿到劳伦斯神父那里去了吗？

乳　　　母　正是。

凯普莱特　好，也许他可以劝告劝告她；真是个乖僻不听话的浪蹄子！

（朱丽叶上）

乳　　　母　瞧她已经忏悔完毕，高高兴兴地回来啦。

凯普莱特　啊，我的倔强的丫头！你荡到什么地方去啦？

朱　丽　叶　我因为自知忤逆不孝，违抗了您的命令，所以特地前去忏悔我的罪过。现在我听从劳伦斯神父的指教，跪在这儿请您宽恕。爸爸，请您宽恕我吧！从此以后，我永远听您的话了。

凯普莱特　去请伯爵来，对他说：我要把婚礼改在明天早上举行。

朱　丽　叶　我在劳伦斯寺里遇见这位少年伯爵；我已经在不超过礼法的范围以内，向他表示过我的爱情了。

凯普莱特　啊，那很好，我很高兴。站起来吧；这样才对。让我见见这伯爵；喂，快去请他过来。多谢上帝，把这位可尊敬的神父赐给我们！我们全城的人都感戴他的

	Now, afore God, this reverend holy friar,
	All our whole city is much bound to him.
JULIET	Nurse, will you go with me into my closet
	To help me sort such needful ornaments
	As you think fit to furnish me to-morrow?
Mother	No, not till Thursday. There is time enough.
CAPULET	Go, nurse, go with her. We'll to church to-morrow.
	[*Exeunt Juliet and Nurse.*]
Mother	We shall be short in our provision.
	'Tis now near night.
CAPULET	Tush, I will stir about,
	And all things shall be well, I warrant thee, wife.
	Go thou to Juliet, help to deck up her.
	I'll not to bed to-night. Let me alone.
	I'll play the housewife for this once. What, ho!
	They are all forth; well, I will walk myself
	To County Paris, to prepare him up
	Against to-morrow. My heart is wondrous light,
	Since this same wayward girl is so reclaim'd.
	[*Exeunt.*]

SCENE III *The same. Juliet's chamber.*

[*Enter Juliet and Nurse.*]

JULIET	Ay, those attires are best; but, gentle nurse,
	I pray thee leave me to myself to-night;
	For I have need of many orisons
	To move the heavens to smile upon my state,
	Which, well thou knowest, is cross and full of sin.

好处。

朱丽叶　奶妈，请你陪我到我的房间里去，帮我检点检点衣饰，看有哪几件可以在明天穿戴。

凯普莱特夫人　不，还是到星期四再说吧，急什么呢？

凯普莱特　去，奶妈，陪她去。我们一定明天上教堂。（朱丽叶及乳母下）

凯普莱特夫人　我们现在预备起来怕来不及；天已经快黑了。

凯普莱特　胡说！我现在就动手起来，你瞧着吧，太太，到明天一定什么都安排得好好的。你快去帮朱丽叶打扮打扮；我今天晚上不睡了，让我一个人在这儿做一次管家妇。喂！喂！这些人一个都不在。好，让我自己跑到帕里斯那里去，叫他准备明天做新郎。这个倔强的孩子现在回心转意，真叫我高兴得了不得。（各下）

第三场　同前。朱丽叶的卧室

（朱丽叶及乳母上）

朱丽叶　嗯，那些衣服都很好。可是，好奶妈，今天晚上请你不用陪我，因为我还要念许多祷告，求上天宥恕我过去的罪恶，默佑我将来的幸福。

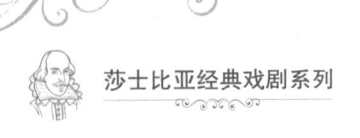

[*Enter Mother.*]

Mother What, are you busy, ho? Need you my help?

JULIET No, madam; we have cull'd such necessaries
As are behoveful for our state to-morrow.
So please you, let me now be left alone,
And let the nurse this night sit up with you;
For I am sure you have your hands full all
In this so sudden business.

Mother Good night.
Get thee to bed, and rest; for thou hast need.
[*Exeunt Mother and Nurse.*]

JULIET Farewell! God knows when we shall meet again.
I have a faint cold fear thrills through my veins
That almost freezes up the heat of life.
I'll call them back again to comfort me.
Nurse! — What should she do here?
My dismal scene I needs must act alone.
Come, vial.
What if this mixture do not work at all?
Shall I be married then to-morrow morning?
No, No! This shall forbid it. Lie thou there.
[*Lays down a dagger.*]
What if it be a poison which the friar
Subtilly hath minist'red to have me dead,
Lest in this marriage he should be dishonour'd
Because he married me before to Romeo?
I fear it is; and yet methinks it should not,
For he hath still been tried a holy man.
How if, when I am laid into the tomb,

（凯普莱特夫人上）

凯普莱特夫人　啊！你正在忙着吗？要不要我帮你？

朱　丽　叶　不，母亲；我们已经选择好了明天需用的一切，所以现在请您让我一个人在这儿吧；让奶妈今天晚上陪着您不睡，因为我相信这次事情办得太匆促了，您一定忙得不可开交。

凯普莱特夫人　晚安！早点睡觉，你应该好好休息休息。（凯普莱特夫人及乳母下）

朱　丽　叶　再会！上帝知道我们将在什么时候相见。我觉得仿佛有一阵寒颤刺激着我的血液，简直要把生命的热流冻结起来似的；待我叫她们回来安慰安慰我。奶妈！——要她到这儿来干什么？这凄惨的场面必须让我一个人扮演。来，药瓶。要是这药水不发生效力呢？那么我明天早上就必须结婚吗？不，不，这把刀会阻止我；你躺在那儿吧。（将匕首置枕边）也许这

I wake before the time that Romeo
Come to redeem me? There's a fearful point!
Shall I not then be stifled in the vault,
To whose foul mouth no healthsome air breathes in,
And there die strangled ere my Romeo comes?
Or, if I live, is it not very like
The horrible conceit of death and night,
Together with the terror of the place
As in a vault, an ancient receptacle
Where for this many hundred years the bones
Of all my buried ancestors are pack'd;
Where bloody Tybalt, yet but green in earth,
Lies fest'ring in his shroud; where, as they say,
At some hours in the night spirits resort —
Alack, alack, is it not like that I,
So early waking — what with loathsome smells,
And shrieks like mandrakes torn out of the earth,
That living mortals, hearing them, run mad —
O, if I wake, shall I not be distraught,
Environed with all these hideous fears,
And madly play with my forefathers' joints,
And pluck the mangled Tybalt from his shroud,
And, in this rage, with some great kinsman's bone
As with a club dash out my desp'rate brains?
O, look! methinks I see my cousin's ghost
Seeking out Romeo, that did spit his body
Upon a rapier's point. Stay, Tybalt, stay!
Romeo, I come! this do I drink to thee.

[*She drinks and falls upon her bed within the curtains.*]

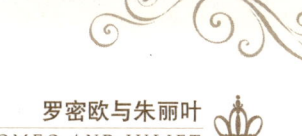

瓶里是毒药，那神父因为已经替我和罗密欧证婚，现在我再跟别人结婚，恐怕损害他的名誉，所以有意骗我服下去毒死我；我怕也许会有这样的事；可是他一向是众所公认的道高德重的人，我想大概不至于；我不能抱着这样卑劣的思想。要是我在坟墓里醒了过来，罗密欧还没有到来把我救出去呢？这倒是很可怕的一点！那时我不是要在终年透不进一丝新鲜空气的地窟里活活闷死，等不到我的罗密欧到来吗？即使不闷死，那死亡和长夜的恐怖，那古墓中阴森的气象，几百年来，我祖先的尸骨都堆积在那里，入土未久的提伯尔特蒙着他的殓衾，正在那里腐烂；人家说，一到晚上，鬼魂便会归返他们的墓穴；唉！唉！要是我太早醒来，这些恶臭的气味，这些使人听了会发疯的凄厉的叫声；啊！要是我醒来，周围都是这种吓人的东西，我不会心神迷乱，疯狂地抚弄着我的祖宗的骨骼，把肢体溃烂的提伯尔特拖出了他的殓衾吗？在这样疯狂的状态中，我不会拾起一根老祖宗的骨头来，当作一根棍子，打破我的发昏的头颅吗？啊，瞧！那不是提伯尔特的鬼魂，正在那里追赶罗密欧，报复他的一剑之仇吗？等一等，提伯尔特，等一等！罗密欧，我来了！我为你干了这一杯！（倒在幕内的床上）

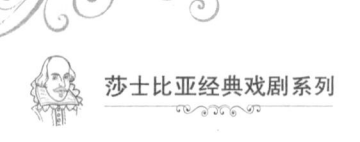

SCENE IV The same. Capulet's house.

[*Enter Lady of the House and Nurse.*]

Lady Hold, take these keys and fetch more spices, nurse.
Nurse They call for dates and quinces in the pastry.

[*Enter Old Capulet.*]

CAPULET Come, stir, stir, stir! The second cock hath crow'd,
The curfew bell hath rung, 'tis three o'clock.
Look to the bak'd meats, good Angelica;
Spare not for cost.

Nurse Go, you cot-quean, go,
Get you to bed! Faith, you'll be sick to-morrow
For this night's watching.

CAPULET No, not a whit. What, I have watch'd ere now
All night for lesser cause, and ne'er been sick.

Lady Ay, you have been a mouse-hunt in your time;
But I will watch you from such watching now.

[*Exeunt Lady and Nurse.*]

CAULET A jealous hood, a jealous hood!

[*Enter three or four Fellows, with spits and logs and baskets.*]

What is there? Now, fellow,

Fellow Things for the cook, sir; but I know not what.
CAPULET Make haste, make haste. [*Exit Fellow.*]
Sirrah, fetch drier logs.
Call Peter; he will show thee where they are.

Fellow I have a head, sir, that will find out logs
And never trouble Peter for the matter.

第四场　同前。凯普莱特家中厅堂

（凯普莱特夫人及乳母上）

凯普莱特夫人　奶妈，把这串钥匙拿去，再拿一点香料来。

乳　　母　点心房里在喊着要枣子和榅桲呢。

（凯普莱特上）

凯 普 莱 特　来，赶紧点儿，赶紧点儿！鸡已经叫了第二次，晚钟已经打过，到三点钟了。好安吉丽加，当心看看肉饼有没有烤焦。多花几个钱没有关系。

乳　　母　走开，走开，女人家的事用不着您多管；快去睡吧，今天忙了一个晚上，明天又要害病了。

凯 普 莱 特　不，哪儿的话！嘿，我为了没要紧的事，也曾经整夜不睡，几曾害过病来？

凯普莱特夫人　对啦，你从前也是惯偷女人的夜猫儿，可是现在我却不放你出去胡闹啦。（凯普莱特夫人及乳母下）

凯 普 莱 特　真是个醋娘子！真是个醋娘子！

（三四仆人持炙叉、木柴及篮上）

喂，这是什么东西？

仆　　甲　老爷，都是拿去给厨子的，我也不知道是什么东西。

凯 普 莱 特　赶紧点儿，赶紧点儿。（仆甲下）喂，木头要拣干燥点儿的，你去问彼得，他可以告诉你什么地方有。

仆　　乙　老爷，我自己也长着眼睛会拣木头，用不着麻烦彼得。

CAPULET	Mass, and well said; a merry whoreson, ha!
	Thou shalt be loggerhead. [*Exit Fellow.*] Good faith, 'tis day!
	The County will be here with music straight,
	For so he said he would.
	[*Play music.*]
	I hear him near.
	Nurse! Wife! What, ho! What, nurse, I say!
	[*Enter Nurse.*]
	Go waken Juliet; go and trim her up.
	I'll go and chat with Paris. Hie, make haste,
	Make haste! The bridegroom he is come already:
	Make haste, I say.
	[*Exeunt.*]

SCENE V   *The same. Juliet's chamber.*

[*Enter Nurse.*]

Nurse	Mistress! what, mistress! Juliet! Fast, I warrant her, she.
	Why, lamb! why, lady! Fie, you slug-abed!
	Why, love, I say! madam! sweetheart! Why, bride!
	What, not a word? You take your pennyworths now!
	Sleep for a week; for the next night, I warrant,
	The County Paris hath set up his rest
	That you shall rest but little, God forgive me!
	Marry, and amen. How sound is she asleep!
	I needs must wake her. Madam, madam, madam!
	Ay, let the County take you in your bed!
	He'll fright you up, i'faith. Will it not be?

凯普莱特 嘿，倒说得有理，这个淘气的小杂种！（仆乙下）哎哟！天已经亮了；伯爵就要带着乐工来了，他说过的。（内乐声）我听见他已经走近了。奶妈！妻子！喂，喂！喂，奶妈呢？

（乳母重上）

快去叫朱丽叶起来，把她打扮打扮；我要去跟帕里斯谈天去了。快去，快去，赶紧点儿；新郎已经来了；赶紧点儿！（各下）

第五场 同前。朱丽叶的卧室

（乳母上）

乳　母 小姐！喂，小姐！朱丽叶！她准是睡熟了。喂，小羊！喂，小姐！哼，你这懒丫头！喂，亲亲！小姐！心肝！喂，新娘！怎么！一声也不响？现在尽你睡去，尽你睡一个星期；到今天晚上，帕里斯伯爵可不让你安安静静休息一会儿了。上帝饶恕我，阿门，她睡得多熟！我必须叫她醒来。小姐！小姐！小姐！好，让那伯爵自己到你床上来吧，那时你可要吓得跳起来了，是不是？怎么！衣服都穿好了，又重新睡下去吗？我必须

[*Draws aside the curtains.*]

What, dress'd, and in your clothes, and down again?

I must needs wake you. Lady! lady! lady!

Alas, alas! Help, help! My lady's dead!

O weraday that ever I was born!

Some aqua-vitae, ho! My lord! my lady!

[*Enter Mother.*]

Mother	What noise is here?
Nurse	O lamentable day!
Mother	What is the matter?
Nurse	Look, look ! O heavy day!
Mother	O me, O me! My child, my only life!

Revive, look up, or I will die with thee!

Help, help! Call help.

[*Enter Father.*]

Father	For shame, bring Juliet forth; her lord is come.
Nurse	She's dead, deceas'd; she's dead! Alack the day!
Mother	Alack the day, she's dead, she's dead, she's dead!
CAPULET	Ha! let me see her. Out alas! she's cold,

Her blood is settled, and her joints are stiff;

Life and these lips have long been separated.

Death lies on her like an untimely frost

Upon the sweetest flower of all the field.

Nurse	O lamentable day!
Mother	O woeful time!
CAPULET	Death, that hath ta'en her hence to make me wail,

Ties up my tongue and will not let me speak.

[*Enter Friar Laurence and the County Paris, with Musicians.*]

把你叫醒。小姐！小姐！小姐！哎哟！哎哟！救命！救命！我的小姐死了！哎哟！我还活着做什么！喂，拿一点酒来！老爷！太太！

（凯普莱特夫人上）

凯普莱特夫人　吵什么？

乳　　母　　哎哟，好伤心啊！

凯普莱特夫人　什么事？

乳　　母　　瞧，瞧！哎哟，好伤心啊！

凯普莱特夫人　哎哟，哎哟！我的孩子，我的唯一的生命！醒来！睁开你的眼睛来！你死了，叫我怎么活得下去？救命！救命！大家来啊！

（凯普莱特上）

凯 普 莱 特　还不送朱丽叶出来，她的新郎已经来啦。

乳　　母　　她死了，死了，她死了！哎哟，伤心啊！

凯普莱特夫人　唉！她死了，她死了，她死了！

凯 普 莱 特　嘿！让我瞧瞧。哎哟！她身上冰冷的；她的血液已经停止不流，她的手脚都硬了；她的嘴唇里已经没有了生命的气息；死像一阵未秋先降的寒霜，摧残了这一朵最鲜嫩的娇花。

乳　　母　　哎哟，好伤心啊！

凯普莱特夫人　哎哟，好苦啊！

凯 普 莱 特　死神夺去了我的孩子，他使我悲伤得说不出话来。

（劳伦斯神父、帕里斯及乐工等上）

Friar	Come, is the bride ready to go to church?
CAPULET	Ready to go, but never to return.
	O son, the night before thy wedding day
	Hath Death lain with thy wife. See, there she lies,
	Flower as she was, deflowered by him.
	Death is my son-in-law, Death is my heir;
	My daughter he hath wedded. I will die
	And leave him all. Life, living, all is Death's.
PARIS	Have I thought long to see this morning's face,
	And doth it give me such a sight as this?
Mother	Accurs'd, unhappy, wretched, hateful day!
	Most miserable hour that e'er time saw
	In lasting labour of his pilgrimage!
	But one, poor one, one poor and loving child,
	But one thing to rejoice and solace in,
	And cruel Death hath catch'd it from my sight!
Nurse	O woe! O woeful, woeful, woeful day!
	Most lamentable day, most woeful day
	That ever ever I did yet behold!
	O day! O day! O day! O hateful day!
	Never was seen so black a day as this.
	O woeful day! O woeful day!
PARIS	Beguil'd, divorced, wronged, spited, slain!
	Most detestable Death, by thee beguil'd,
	By cruel cruel thee quite overthrown!
	O love! O life! not life, but love in death!
CAPULET	Despis'd, distressed, hated, martyr'd, kill'd!
	Uncomfortable time, why cam'st thou now
	To murther, murther our solemnity?

劳 伦 斯	来,新娘有没有预备好上教堂去?
凯普莱特	她已经预备动身,可是这一去再不回来了。啊,贤婿!死神已经在你新婚的前夜降临到你妻子的身上。她躺在那里,像一朵被他摧残了的鲜花。死神是我的新婿,是我的后嗣,他已经娶走了我的女儿。我也快要死了,把我的一切都传给他;我的生命财产,一切都是死神的!
帕 里 斯	难道我眼巴巴望到天明,却让我看见这一个凄惨的情景吗?
凯普莱特夫人	倒霉的、不幸的、可恨的日子!永无休止的时间的运行中的一个顶悲惨的时辰!我就生了这一个孩子,这一个可怜的疼爱的孩子,她是我唯一的宝贝和安慰,现在却被残酷的死神从我眼前夺了去啦!
乳 母	好苦啊!好苦的、好苦的、好苦的日子啊!我这一生一世里顶伤心的日子,顶凄凉的日子!哎哟,这个日子!这个可恨的日子!从来不曾见过这样倒霉的日子!好苦的、好苦的日子啊!
帕 里 斯	最可恨的死,你欺骗了我,杀害了她,拆散了我们的良缘,一切都被残酷的、残酷的你破坏了!啊!爱人!啊,我的生命!没有生命,只有被死亡吞噬了的爱情!
凯普莱特	悲痛的命运,为什么你要来打破、打破我们的盛礼?儿啊!儿啊!我的灵魂,你死了!你已经不是我的孩

	O child! O child! my soul, and not my child!
	Dead art thou, dead! alack, my child is dead,
	And with my child my joys are buried!
Friar	Peace, ho, for shame! Confusion's cure lives not
	In these confusions. Heaven and yourself
	Had part in this fair maid! now heaven hath all,
	And all the better is it for the maid.
	Your part in her you could not keep from death,
	But heaven keeps his part in eternal life.
	The most you sought was her promotion,
	For 'twas your heaven she should be advanc'd;
	And weep ye now, seeing she is advanc'd
	Above the clouds, as high as heaven itself?
	O, in this love, you love your child so ill
	That you run mad, seeing that she is well.
	She's not well married that lives married long,
	But she's best married that dies married young.
	Dry up your tears and stick your rosemary
	On this fair corse, and, as the custom is,
	In all her best array bear her to church;
	For though fond nature bids us all lament,
	Yet nature's tears are reason's merriment.
CAPULET	All things that we ordained festival
	Turn from their office to black funeral —
	Our instruments to melancholy bells,
	Our wedding cheer to a sad burial feast;
	Our solemn hymns to sullen dirges change;
	Our bridal flowers serve for a buried corse;
	And all things change them to the contrary.

子了！死了！唉！我的孩子死了，我的快乐也随着我的孩子埋葬了！

劳伦斯　静下来！不害羞吗？你们这样乱哭乱叫是无济于事的。上天和你们共有着这一个好女儿；现在她已经完全属于上天所有，这是她的幸福，因为你们不能使她的肉体避免死亡，上天却能使她的灵魂得到永生。你们竭力替她找寻一个美满的前途，因为你们的幸福是寄托在她的身上；现在她高高地升上云中去了，你们却为她哭泣吗？啊！你们瞧着她享受最大的幸福，却这样发疯一样号啕叫喊，这可以算是真爱你们的女儿吗？活着，嫁了人，一直到老，这样的婚姻有什么乐趣呢？在年轻时候结了婚而死去，才是最幸福不过的。揩干你们的眼泪，把你们的香花散布在这美丽的尸体上，按照着习惯，把她穿着盛装抬到教堂里去。愚痴的天性虽然使我们伤心痛哭，可是在理智眼中，这些天性的眼泪却是可笑的。

凯普莱特　我们本来为了喜庆预备好的一切，现在都要变成悲哀的殡礼；我们的乐器要变成忧郁的丧钟，我们的婚筵要变成凄凉的丧席，我们的赞美诗要变成沉痛的挽歌，新娘手里的鲜花要放在坟墓中殉葬，一切都要相反而行。

Friar	Sir, go you in; and, madam, go with him;
	And go, Sir Paris. Every one prepare
	To follow this fair corse unto her grave.
	The heavens do low'r upon you for some ill;
	Move them no more by crossing their high will.
	[*Exeunt. Manent Musicians and Nurse.*]
First Musician	Faith, we may put up our pipes and be gone.
Nurse	Honest good fellows, ah, put up, put up!
	For well you know this is a pitiful case. [*Exit.*]
First Musician	Ay, by my troth, the case may be amended.
	[*Enter Peter.*]
PETER	Musicians, O, musicians, 'Heart's ease', 'Heart's ease'!
	O, and you will have me live, play 'Heart's ease'.
First Musician	Why 'Heart's ease'?
PETER	O, musicians, because my heart itself plays 'My heart is full of woe.'
	O, play me some merry dump to comfort me.
First Musician	Not a dump we! 'Tis no time to play now.
PETER	You will not then?
First Musician	No.
PETER	I will then give it you soundly.
First Musician	What will you give us?
PETER	No money, on my faith, but the gleek. I will give you the minstrel.
First Musician	Then will I give you the serving-creature.
PETER	Then will I lay the serving-creature's dagger on your pate.
	I will carry no crotchets. I'll re you, I'll fa you. Do you note me?

劳伦斯　凯普莱特先生，您进去吧；夫人，您陪他进去；帕里斯伯爵，您也去吧；大家准备送这具美丽的尸体下葬。上天的愤怒已经降临在你们身上，不要再违拂他的意旨，招致更大的灾祸。

（凯普莱特夫妇、帕里斯、劳伦斯同下）

乐工甲　真的，咱们也可以收起笛子走啦。

乳母　啊！好兄弟们，收起来吧，收起来吧；这真是一场伤心的横祸！（下）

乐工甲　唉，我巴不得这事有什么办法补救才好。

（彼得上）

彼得　乐工！啊！乐工，《心里的安乐》《心里的安乐》！啊！替我奏一曲《心里的安乐》，否则我要活不下去了。

乐工甲　为什么要奏《心里的安乐》呢？

彼得　啊！乐工，因为我的心在那里唱着《我心里充满了忧伤》。啊！替我奏一支快活的歌儿，安慰安慰我吧。

乐工甲　不奏不奏，现在不是奏乐的时候。

彼得　那么你们不奏吗？

乐工甲　不奏。

彼得　那么我就给你们——

乐工甲　你给我们什么？

彼得　我可不给你们钱，哼！我要给你们一顿骂；我骂你们是一群卖唱的叫花子。

乐工甲　那么我就骂你是个下贱的奴才。

彼得　那么我就把奴才的刀搁在你们的头颅上。我决不含糊：不是高音，就是低调，你们听见吗？

First Musician	An you re us and fa us, you note us.
Second Musician	Pray you put up your dagger, and put out your wit.
PETER	Then have at you with my wit! I will dry-beat you with an iron wit, and put up my iron dagger. Answer me like men.

>'When griping grief the heart doth wound,
>And doleful dumps the mind oppress,
>Then music with her silver sound'

	Why 'silver sound'? Why 'music with her silver sound'?
	What say you, Simon Catling?
First Musician	Marry, sir, because silver hath a sweet sound.
PETER	Pretty! What say you, Hugh Rebeck?
Second Musician	I say 'silver sound' because musicians sound for silver.
PETER	Pretty too! What say you, James Soundpost?
Third Musician	Faith, I know not what to say.
PETER	O, I cry you mercy! you are the singer. I will say for you.
	It is 'music with her silver sound' because musicians have no gold for sounding.
	'Then music with her silver sound
	With speedy help doth lend redress.' [*Exit.*]
First Musician	What a pestilent knave is this same?
Second Musician	Hang him, Jack! Come, we'll in here, tarry for the mourners, and stay dinner.

[*Exeunt.*]

乐工甲　什么高音低调，你倒还得懂这一套。

乐工乙　且慢，君子动口，小人动手。

彼　得　好，那么让我用舌剑唇枪杀得你们抱头鼠窜。有本领的，回答我这一个问题：

　　　　悲哀伤痛着心灵，

　　　　忧郁萦绕在胸怀，

　　　　惟有音乐的银声——

　　　　为什么说"银声"？为什么说"音乐的银声"？西门·凯特林，你怎么说？

乐工甲　因为银子的声音很好听。

彼　得　说得好！休利·培克，你怎么说？

乐工乙　因为乐工奏乐的目的，是想人家赏他一些银子。

彼　得　说得好！詹姆士·桑德普斯特，你怎么说？

乐工丙　不瞒你说，我可不知道应当怎么说。

彼　得　啊！对不起，你是只会唱唱歌的；我替你说了吧：因为乐工尽管奏乐奏到老死，也换不到一些金子。惟有音乐的银声，可以把烦闷推开。（下）

乐工甲　真是个讨厌的家伙！

乐工乙　该死的奴才！来，咱们且慢回去，等吊客来的时候吹奏两声，吃他们一顿饭再走。（同下）

Act V

SCENE I Mantua. A street.

[*Enter Romeo.*]

ROMEO   If I may trust the flattering math of sleep
My dreams presage some joyful news at hand.
My bosom's lord sits lightly in his throne,
And all this day an unaccustom'd spirit
Lifts me above the ground with cheerful thoughts.
I dreamt my lady came and found me dead
(Strange dream that gives a dead man leave to think!)
And breath'd such life with kisses in my lips
That I reviv'd and was an emperor.
Ah me! How sweet is love itself possess'd,
When but love's shadows are so rich in joy!
[*Enter Romeo's man Balthasar, booted.*]
News from Verona! How now, Balthasar?
Dost thou not bring me letters from the friar?
How doth my lady? Is my father well?
How fares my Juliet? That I ask again,
For nothing can be ill if she be well.

Man   Then she is well, and nothing can be ill.
Her body sleeps in Capel's monument,
And her immortal part with angels lives.
I saw her laid low in her kindred's vault
And presently took post to tell it you.
O, pardon me for bringing these ill news,

第五幕

第一场　曼图亚。街道

（罗密欧上）

罗密欧　要是梦寐中的幻景果然可以代表真实，那么我的梦预兆着将有好消息到来；我觉得心君宁恬，整日里有一种向所没有的精神，用快乐的思想把我从地面上飘扬起来。我梦见我的爱人来看见我死了——奇怪的梦，一个死人也会思想！——她吻着我，把生命吐进了我的嘴唇里，于是我复活了，并且成为一个君王。唉！仅仅是爱的影子，已经给人这样丰富的欢乐，要是能占有爱的本身，那该有多么甜蜜！

（鲍尔萨泽上）

从维罗纳来的消息！啊，鲍尔萨泽！不是神父叫你带信来给我吗？我的爱人怎样？我父亲好吗？我再问你一遍，我的朱丽叶安好吗？因为只要她安好，一定什么都是好好的。

鲍尔萨泽　那么都是安好的，什么都是好好的；她的身体长眠在凯普莱特家的坟茔里，她的不死的灵魂和天使们在一起。我看见她下葬在她亲族的墓穴里，所以立刻飞马前来告诉您。啊，少爷！恕我带了这恶消息来，因为

	Since you did leave it for my office, sir.
ROMEO	Is it e'en so? Then I defy you, stars!
	Thou knowest my lodging. Get me ink and paper
	And hire posthorses. I will hence to-night.
Man	I do beseech you, sir, have patience.
	Your looks are pale and wild and do import
	Some misadventure.
ROMEO	Tush, thou art deceiv'd.
	Leave me and do the thing I bid thee do.
	Hast thou no letters to me from the friar?
Man	No, my good lord.
ROMEO	No matter. Get thee gone
	And hire those horses. I'll be with thee straight.

[*Exit Balthar.*]

Well, Juliet, I will lie with thee to-night.
Let's see for means. O mischief, thou art swift
To enter in the thoughts of desperate men!
I do remember an apothecary,
And hereabouts 'a dwells, which late I noted
In tatt'red weeds, with overwhelming brows,
Culling of simples. Meagre were his looks,
Sharp misery had worn him to the bones;
And in his needy shop a tortoise hung,
An alligator stuff'd, and other skins
Of ill-shaped fishes; and about his shelves
A beggarly account of empty boxes,
Green earthen pots, bladders, and musty seeds
Remnants of packthread, and old cakes of roses
Were thinly scattered, to make up a show.

这是您吩咐我做的事。

罗　密　欧　有这样的事！命运，我诅咒你！——你知道我的住处；给我买些纸笔，雇下两匹快马，我今天晚上就要动身。

鲍尔萨泽　少爷，请您宽心一下；您的脸色惨白而仓皇，恐怕是不吉之兆。

罗　密　欧　胡说，你看错了。快去，把我叫你做的事赶快办好。神父没有叫你带信给我吗？

鲍尔萨泽　没有，我的好少爷。

罗　密　欧　算了，你去吧，把马匹雇好了；我就来找你。（鲍尔萨泽下）好，朱丽叶，今晚我要睡在你的身旁。让我想个办法。啊，罪恶的念头！你会多么快钻进一个绝望者的心里！我想起了一个卖药的人，他的铺子就开设在附近，我曾经看见他穿着一身破烂的衣服，皱着眉头在那儿拣药草；他的形状十分消瘦，贫苦把他熬煎得只剩一把骨头；他的寒伧的铺子里挂着一只乌龟，一头剥制的鳄鱼，还有几张形状丑陋的鱼皮；他的架子上稀疏地散放着几只空匣子、绿色的瓦罐、一些胞囊和发霉的种子、几段包扎的麻绳，还有几块陈年的干玫瑰花，作为聊胜于无

Noting this penury, to myself I said,
'An if a man did need a poison now
Whose sale is present death in Mantua,
Here lives a caitiff wretch would sell it him.'
O, this same thought did but forerun my need,
And this same needy man must sell it me.
As I remember, this should be tho house.
Being holiday, the beggar's shop is shut.
What, ho! apothecary!
[*Enter Apothecary.*]

Apothecary Who calls so loud?

ROMEO Come hither, man. I see that thou art poor.
Hold, there is forty ducats. Let me have
A dram of poison, such soon-speeding gear
As will disperse itself through all the veins
That the life-weary taker may fall dead,
And that the trunk may be discharg'd of breath
As violently as hasty powder fir'd
Doth hurry from the facal cannon's womb.

Apothecary Such mortal drugs I have, but Mantua's law
Is death to any he that utters them.

ROMEO Art thou so bare and full of wretchedness
And fearest to die? Famine is in thy cheeks,
Need and oppression starveth in thy eyes,
Contempt and beggary hangs upon thy back:
The world is not thy friend, nor the world's law;
The world affords no law to make thee rich;
Then be not poor, but break it and take this.

Apothecary My poverty but not my will consents.

的点缀。看到这一种寒酸的样子，我就对自己说，在曼图亚城里，谁出卖了毒药是会立刻处死的，可是倘有谁现在需要毒药，这儿有一个可怜的奴才会卖给他。啊！不料我这一个思想，竟会预兆着我自己的需要，这个穷汉的毒药却要卖给我。我记得这里就是他的铺子；今天是假日，所以这叫花子没有开门。喂！卖药的！

（卖药人上）

卖　药　人　谁在高声叫喊？

罗　密　欧　过来，朋友。我瞧你很穷，这儿是四十块钱，请你给我一点能够迅速致命的毒药，厌倦于生命的人一服下去便会散入全身的血管，立刻停止呼吸而死去，就像火药从炮膛里放射出去一样快。

卖　药　人　这种致命的毒药我是有的；可是曼图亚的法律严禁出卖，出卖的人是要处死刑的。

罗　密　欧　难道你这样穷苦，还怕死吗？饥寒的痕迹刻在你的面颊上，贫乏和迫害在你的眼睛里射出了饿火，轻蔑和卑贱重压在你的背上；这世间不是你的朋友，这世间的法律也保护不到你，没有人为你定下一条法律使你富有；那么你何必苦耐着贫穷呢？违犯了法律，把这些钱收下吧。

卖　药　人　我的贫穷答应了你，可是那是违反我的良心的。

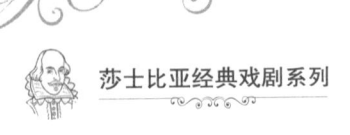

ROMEO	I pay thy poverty and not thy will.
Apothecary	Put this in any liquid thing you will
	And drink it off, and if you had the strength
	Of twenty men, it would dispatch you straight.
ROMEO	There is thy gold — worse poison to men's souls,
	Doing more murther in this loathsome world,
	Than these poor compounds that thou mayst not sell.
	I sell thee poison; thou hast sold me none.
	Farewell. Buy food and get thyself in flesh.
	Come, cordial and not poison, go with me
	To Juliet's grave; for there must I use thee.
	[*Exeunt.*]

SCENE II *Verona. Friar Laurence's cell.*

[*Enter Friar John to Friar Laurence.*]

JOHN	Holy Franciscan friar, brother, ho!
	[*Enter Friar Laurence.*]
LAURENCE	This same should be the voice of Friar John.
	Welcome from Mantua. What says Romeo?
	Or, if his mind be writ, give me his letter.
JOHN	Going to find a barefoot brother out,
	One of our order, to associate me
	Here in this city visiting the sick,
	And finding him, the searchers of the town,
	Suspecting that we both were in a house
	Where the infectious pestilence did reign,
	Seal'd up the doors, and would not let us forth,
	So that my speed to Mantua there was stay'd.

罗密欧　　我的钱是给你的贫穷，不是给你的良心的。

卖药人　　把这一服药放在无论什么饮料里喝下去，即使你有二十个人的气力，也会立刻送命。

罗密欧　　这儿是你的钱，那才是害人灵魂的更坏的毒药，在这万恶的世界上，它比你那些不准贩卖的微贱的药品更会杀人；你没有把毒药卖给我，是我把毒药卖给你。再见；买些吃的东西，把你自己喂得胖一点。——来，你不是毒药，你是替我解除痛苦的仙丹，我要带着你到朱丽叶的坟上去，少不得要借重你一下哩。（各下）

第二场　维罗纳。劳伦斯神父的寺院

（约翰神父上）

约　翰　　喂！师兄在哪里？

（劳伦斯神父上）

劳伦斯　　这是约翰师弟的声音。欢迎你从曼图亚回来！罗密欧怎么说？要是他的意思在信里写明，那么把他的信给我吧。

约　翰　　我临走的时候，因为要找一个同门的师弟作我的同伴，他正在这城里访问病人，不料给本地巡逻的人看见了，疑心我们走进了一家染着瘟疫的人家，把门封锁住了，不让我们出来，所以耽误了我的曼图亚之行。

LAURENCE	Who bare my letter, then, to Romeo?
JOHN	I could not send it — here it is again —
	Nor get a messenger to bring it thee,
	So fearful were they of infection.
LAURENCE	Unhappy fortune! By my brotherhood,
	The letter was not nice, but full of charge,
	Of dear import; and the neglecting it
	May do much danger. Friar John, go hence,
	Get me an iron crow and bring it straight
	Unto my cell.
	[*Exit.*]
JOHN	Brother, I'll go and bring it thee.
LAURENCE	Now, must I to the monument alone.
	Within this three hours will fair Juliet wake.
	She will beshrew me much that Romeo
	Hath had no notice of these accidents;
	But I will write again to Mantua,
	And keep her at my cell till Romeo come
	Poor living corse, clos'd in a dead man's tomb!
	[*Exit.*]

SCENE III　*The same. A churchyard; in it the monument of the Capulets.*

[*Enter Paris and his Page with flowers and a torch.*]

PARIS	Give me thy torch, boy. Hence, and stand aloof.
	Yet put it out, for I would not be seen.
	Under yond yewtree lay thee all along,
	Holding thine ear close to the hollow ground.

劳伦斯　那么谁把我的信送去给罗密欧了？
约　翰　我没有法子把它送出去，现在我又把它带回来了；因为他们害怕瘟疫传染，也没有人愿意把它送还给你。
劳伦斯　糟了！这封信不是等闲，性质十分重要，把它耽误下来，也许会引起极大的灾祸。约翰师弟，你快去给我找一柄铁锄，立刻带到这儿来。
约　翰　好师兄，我去给你拿来。（下）
劳伦斯　现在我必须独自到墓地里去；在这三小时之内，朱丽叶就会醒来，她因为罗密欧不曾知道这些事情，一定会责怪我。我现在要再写一封信到曼图亚去，让她留在我的寺院里，直等罗密欧到来。可怜的没有死的尸体，幽闭在一座死人的坟墓里！（下）

第三场　同前。凯普莱特家坟茔所在的墓地

（帕里斯及侍童携鲜花、火炬上）

帕里斯　孩子，把你的火把给我；走开，站在远远的地方；还是灭了吧，我不愿给人看见。你到那边的紫杉树底下直躺下来，把你的耳朵贴着中空的地面，地下挖了许

	So shall no foot upon the churchyard tread
	(Being loose, unfirm, with digging up of graves)
	But thou shalt hear it. Whistle then to me,
	As signal that thou hear'st something approach.
	Give me those flowers. Do as I bid thee, go.
Page	[*Aside.*] I am almost afraid to stand alone
	Here in the churchyard; yet I will adventure. [*Retires.*]
PARIS	Sweet flower, with flowers thy bridal bed I strew
	(O woe! thy canopy is dust and stones)
	Which with sweet water nightly I will dew;
	Or, wanting that, with tears distill'd by moans.
	The obsequies that I for thee will keep
	Nightly shall be to strew, thy grave and weep.
	[*Whistle Boy.*]
	The boy gives warning something doth approach.
	What cursed foot wanders this way to-night
	To cross my obsequies and tree love's rite?
	What, with a torch? Muffle me, night, awhile. [*Retires.*]
	[*Enter Romeo, and Balthasar with a torch, a mattock, and a crow of iron.*]
ROMEO	Give me that mattock and the wrenching iron.
	Hold, take this letter. Early in the morning
	See thou deliver it to my lord and father.
	Give me the light. Upon thy life I charge thee,
	Whate'er thou hearest or seest, stand all aloof
	And do not interrupt me in my course.
	Why I descend into this bed of death
	Is partly to behold my lady's face,
	But chiefly to take thence from her dead finger

多墓穴，土是松的，要是有踉跄的脚步走到坟地上来，你准听得见；要是听见有什么声息，便吹一个唿哨通知我。把那些花给我。照我的话做去，走吧。

侍　　童　（旁白）我简直不敢独自一个人站在这墓地上，可是我要硬着头皮试一下。（退后）

帕　里　斯　这些鲜花替你铺盖新床；
惨啊，一朵娇红永委沙尘！
我要用沉痛的热泪淋浪，
和着香水浇溉你的芳坟；
夜夜到你墓前散花哀泣，
这一段相思啊永无消歇！（侍童吹口哨）
这孩子在警告我有人来了。哪一个该死的家伙在这晚上到这儿来打扰我在爱人墓前的凭吊？什么！还拿着火炬来吗？——让我躲在一旁看看他的动静。（退后）

（罗密欧及鲍尔萨泽持火炬锹锄等上）

罗　密　欧　把那锄头跟铁钳给我。且慢，拿着这封信；等天一亮，你就把它送给我的父亲。把火把给我。听好我的吩咐，无论你听见什么瞧见什么，都只好远远地站着不许动，免得妨碍我的事情；要是动一动，我就要你的命。我之所以要跑下这个坟墓里去，一部分的原因是要探望探望我的爱人，可是主要的理由却是要从她的手指上取下一个宝贵的指环，因为我有一个很重要

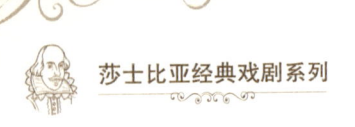

	A precious ring — a ring that I must use
	In dear employment. Therefore hence, be gone.
	But if thou, jealous, dost return to pry
	In what I farther shall intend to do,
	By heaven, I will tear thee joint by joint
	And strew this hungry churchyard with thy limbs.
	The time and my intents are savage — wild,
	More fierce and more inexorable far
	Than empty tigers or the roaring sea.
Man	I will be gone, sir, and not trouble you.
ROMEO	So shalt thou show me friendship. Take thou that.
	Live, and be prosperous; and farewell, good fellow.
Man	[*Aside.*] For all this same, I'll hide me hereabout.
	His looks I fear, and his intents I doubt. [*Retires.*]
ROMEO	Thou detestable maw, thou womb of death,
	Gorg'd with the dearest morsel of the earth,
	Thus I enforce thy rotten jaws to open,
	And in despite I'll cram thee with more food.
	[*Romeo opens the tomb.*]
PARIS	This is that banish'd haughty Montague
	That murd'red my love's cousin — with which grief
	It is supposed the fair creature died
	And here is come to do some villanous shame
	To the dead bodies. I will apprehend him.
	Stop thy unhallowed toil, vile Montague!
	Can vengeance be pursu'd further than death?
	Condemned villain, I do apprehend tlee.
	Obey, and go with me; for thou must die.
ROMEO	I must indeed; and therefore came I hither.

的用途。所以你赶快给我走开吧；要是你不相信我的话，胆敢回来窥伺我的行动，那么，我可以对天发誓，我要把你的骨骼一节一节扯下来，让这饥饿的墓地上散满了你的肢体。我现在的心境非常狂野，比饿虎或是咆哮的怒海都要凶猛无情，你可不要惹我性起。

鲍尔萨泽　少爷，我走就是了，决不来打扰您。

罗　密　欧　这才像个朋友。这些钱你拿去，愿你一生幸福。再会，好朋友。

鲍尔萨泽　（旁白）虽然这么说，我还是要躲在附近的地方看着他；他的脸色使我害怕，我不知道他究竟打算做出什么事来。（退后）

罗　密　欧　你无情的泥土，吞噬了世上最可爱的人儿，我要擘开你的馋吻，索性让你再吃一个饱！（将墓门掘开）

帕　里　斯　这就是那个已经被放逐出去的骄横的蒙太古，他杀死了我爱人的表兄，据说她就是因为伤心他的惨死而夭亡的。现在这家伙又要来盗尸发墓了，待我去抓住他。（上前）万恶的蒙太古！停止你的罪恶的工作，难道你杀了他们还不够，还要在死人身上发泄你的仇恨吗？该死的凶徒，赶快束手就捕，跟我见官去！

罗　密　欧　我果然该死，所以才到这儿来。年轻人，不要激怒一

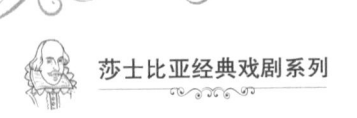

Good gentle youth, tempt not a desp'rate man.
Fly hence and leave me. Think upon these gone;
Let them affright thee. I beseech thee, youth,
Put not another sin upon my head
By urging me to fury. O, be gone!
By heaven, I love thee better than myself,
For I come hither arm'd against myself.
Stay not, be gone. Live, and hereafter say
A madman's mercy bid thee run away.

PARIS I do defy thy conjuration
And apprehend thee for a felon here.

ROMEO Wilt thou provoke me? Then have at thee, boy!
[*They fight.*]

Page O Lord, they fight! I will go call the watch.
[*Exit. Paris falls.*]

PARIS O, I am slain! If thou be merciful,
Open the tomb, lay me with Juliet. [*Dies.*]

ROMEO In faith, I will. Let me peruse this face.
Mercutio's kinsman, noble County Paris!
What said my man when my betossed soul
Did not attend him as we rode? I think
He told me Paris should have married Juliet.
Said he not so? or did I dream it so?
Or am I mad, hearing him talk of Juliet
To think it was so? O, give me thy hand,
One writ with me in sour misfortune's book!
I'll bury thee in a triumphant grave.
A grave? O, no, a lanthorn, slaught'red youth,
For here lies Juliet, and her beauty makes

个不顾死活的人，快快离开我走吧；想想这些死了的人，你也该胆寒了。年轻人，请你不要激动我的怒气，使我再犯一次罪；啊，走吧！我可以对天发誓，我爱你远过于爱我自己，因为我来此的目的，就是要跟自己作对。别留在这儿，走吧；好好留着你的活命，以后也可以对人家说，是一个疯子发了慈悲，叫你逃走的。

帕里斯　我不听你这种鬼话；你是一个罪犯，我要逮捕你。

罗密欧　你一定要激怒我吗？那么好，来，朋友！（二人格斗）

侍童　哎哟，主啊！他们打起来了，我去叫巡逻的人来！（下）

帕里斯　（倒下）啊，我死了！——你倘有几分仁慈，打开墓门来，把我放在朱丽叶的身旁吧！（死）

罗密欧　好，我愿意成全你的志愿。让我瞧瞧他的脸；啊，茂丘西奥的亲戚，尊贵的帕里斯伯爵！当我们一路上骑马而来的时候，我的仆人曾经对我说过几句话，那时我因为心绪烦乱，没有听得进去；他说些什么？好像他告诉我说帕里斯本来预备娶朱丽叶为妻；他不是这样说吗？还是我做过这样的梦？或者还是我神经错乱，听见他说起朱丽叶的名字，所以发生了这一种幻想？啊！把你的手给我，你我都是登录在恶运的黑册上的

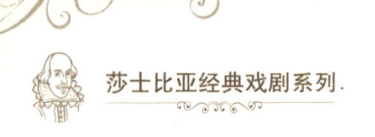

This vault a feasting presence full of light.
Death, lie thou there, by a dead man interr'd.
[*Lays him in the tomb.*]
How oft when men are at the point of death
Have they been merry! which their keepers call
A lightning before death. O, how may I
Call this a lightning? O my love! my wife!
Death, that hath suck'd the honey of thy breath,
Hath had no power yet upon thy beauty.
Thou art not conquer'd. Beauty's ensign yet
Is crimson in thy lips and in thy cheeks,
And death's pale flag is not advanced there.
Tybalt, liest thou there in thy bloody sheet?
O, what more favour can I do to thee
Than with that hand that cut thy youth in twain
To sunder his that was thine enemy?
Forgive me, couisn. Ah, dear Juliet,
Why art thou yet so fair? Shall I believe
That unsubstantial Death is amorous,
And that the lean abhorred monster keeps
Thee here in dark to be his paramour?
For fear of that I still will stay with thee
And never from this palace of dim night
Depart again. Here, here will I remain
With worms that are thy chambermaids. O, here
Will I set up my everlasting rest
And shake the yoke of inauspicious stars
From this world-wearied flesh. Eyes, look your last!
Arms, take your last embrace! and lips, O you

人，我要把你葬在一个胜利的坟墓里；一个坟墓吗？啊，不！被杀害的少年，这是一个灯塔，因为朱丽叶睡在这里，她的美貌使这一个墓窟变成一座充满着光明的欢宴的华堂。死了的人，躺在那儿吧，一个死了的人把你安葬了。（将帕里斯放下墓中）人们临死的时候，往往反会觉得心中愉快，旁观的人便说这是死前的一阵回光返照；啊！这也就是我的回光返照吗？啊，我的爱人！我的妻子！死虽然已经吸去了你呼吸中的芳蜜，却还没有力量摧残你的美貌；你还没有被他征服，你的嘴唇上、面庞上，依然显着红润的美艳，不曾让灰白的死亡进占。提伯尔特，你也裹着你的血淋淋的殓衾躺在那儿吗？啊！你的青春葬送在你仇人的手里，现在我来替你报仇来了，我要亲手杀死那杀害你的人。原谅我吧，兄弟！啊！亲爱的朱丽叶，你为什么仍然这样美丽？难道那虚无的死亡，那枯瘦可憎的妖魔，也是个多情种子，所以把你藏匿在这幽暗的洞府里做他的情妇吗？为了防止这样的事情，我要永远陪伴着你，再不离开这漫漫长夜的幽宫；我要留在这儿，跟你的侍婢，那些蛆虫们在一起。啊！我要在这儿永久安息下来，从我这厌倦人世的凡躯上挣脱恶运的束缚。眼睛，瞧你的最后一眼吧！手臂，做你最后一次的拥抱吧！嘴唇，啊！你呼吸的门户，用一个合法的吻，跟网罗一切的死亡订立一个永久的契约吧！来，苦味的向导，绝望的领港人，现在赶快把你的厌倦于风涛的船舶向那巉岩上冲撞过去吧！为了我的爱人，我干了这一杯！（饮药）啊！卖药的人果然没有骗我，药

  The doors of breath, seal with a righteous kiss

  A dateless bargain to engrossing death!

  Come, bitter conduct; come, unsavoury guide!

  Thou desperate pilot, now at once run on

  The dashing rocks thy seasick weary bark!

  Here's to my love!

  [*Drinks.*]

  O true apothecary!

  Thy drugs are quick. Thus with a kiss I die. Falls.

  [*Enter Friar (Laurence), with lanthorn ,crow, and spade.*]

Friar	Saint Francis be my speed! how oft to-night Have my old feet stumbled at graves! Who's there?
BALTHASAR	Here's one, a friend, and one that knows you well.
Friar	Bliss be upon you! Tell me, good my friend, What torch is yond that vainly lends his light To grubs and eyeless skulls? As I discern, It burneth in the Capels' monument.
BALTHASAR	It doth so, holy sir; and there's my master, One that you love.
Friar	Who is it?
BALTHASAR	Romeo.
Friar	How long hath he been there?
BALTHASAR	Full half an hour.
Friar	Go with me to the vault.
BALTHASAR	I dare not, sir. My master knows not but I am gone hence, And fearfully did menace me with death If I did stay to look on his intents.

性很快地发作了。我就这样在这一吻中死去。（死）

（劳伦斯神父持灯笼、锄、锹自墓地另一端上）

劳　伦　斯　圣法兰西斯保佑我！我这双老脚今天晚上怎么老是在坟堆里绊来跌去的！那边是谁？

鲍尔萨泽　是一个朋友，也是一个跟您熟识的人。

劳　伦　斯　祝福你！告诉我，我的好朋友，那边是什么火把，向蛆虫和没有眼睛的骷髅浪费着它的光明？照我辨认起来，那火把亮着的地方，似乎是凯普莱特家里的坟茔。

鲍尔萨泽　正是，神父；我的主人，您的好朋友，就在那儿。

劳　伦　斯　他是谁？

鲍尔萨泽　罗密欧。

劳　伦　斯　他来多久了？

鲍尔萨泽　足足半点钟。

劳　伦　斯　陪我到墓穴里去。

鲍尔萨泽　我不敢，神父。我的主人不知道我还没有走；他曾经对我严辞恐吓，说要是我留在这儿窥伺他的动静，就要把我杀死。

Friar	Stay then; I'll go alone. Fear comes upon me.
	O, much I fear some ill unthrifty thing.
BALTHASAR	As I did sleep under this yewtree here,
	I dreamt my master and another fought,
	And that my master slew him.
Friar	Romeo!
	Alack, alack, what blood is this which stains
	The stony entrance of this sepulchre?
	What mean these masterless and gory swords
	To lie discolour'd by this place of peace? [Enters the tomb.]
	Romeo! O, pale! Who else? What, Paris too?
	And steep'd in blood? Ah, what an unkind hour
	Is guilty of this lamentable chance! The lady stirs.
	[Juliet rises.]
JULIET	O comfortable friar! where is my lord?
	I do remember well where I should be,
	And there I am. Where is my Romeo? [Noise within.]
Friar	I hear some noise. Lady, Come from that nest
	Of death, contagion, and unnatural sleep.
	A greater power than we can contradict
	Hath thwarted our intents. Come, come away.
	Thy husband in thy bosom there lies dead;
	And Paris too. Come, I'll dispose of thee
	Among a sisterhood of holy nuns.
	Stay not to question, for the watch is coming.
	Come, go, good Juliet. [Noise within again.]
	I dare no longer stay.
JULIET	Go, get thee hence, for I will not away.

劳伦斯	那么你留在这儿,让我一个人去吧。恐惧临到我的身上;啊!我怕会有什么不幸的祸事发生。
鲍尔萨泽	当我在这株紫杉树底下睡了过去的时候,我梦见我的主人跟另外一个人打架,那个人被我的主人杀了。
劳伦斯	(趋前)罗密欧!哎哟!哎哟,这坟墓的石门上染着些什么血迹?在这安静的地方,怎么横放着这两柄无主的血污的刀剑?(进墓)罗密欧!啊,他的脸色这么惨白!还有谁?什么!帕里斯也躺在这儿,浑身浸在血泊里?啊!多么残酷的时辰,造成了这场凄惨的意外!那小姐醒了。(朱丽叶醒)
朱丽叶	啊,善心的神父!我的夫君呢?我记得很清楚我应当在什么地方,现在我正在这地方。我的罗密欧呢?(内喧声)
劳伦斯	我听见有什么声音。小姐,赶快离开这个密布着毒氛腐臭的死亡的巢穴吧;一种我们所不能反抗的力量已经阻挠了我们的计划。来,出去吧。你的丈夫已经在你的怀中死去;帕里斯也死了。来,我可以替你找一处地方出家做尼姑。不要耽误时间盘问我,巡夜的人就要来了。来,好朱丽叶,去吧。(内喧声又起)我不敢再等下去了。
朱丽叶	去,你去吧!我不愿意走。(劳伦斯下)这是什么?

[*Exit Friar.*]
What's here? A cup, clos'd in my true love's hand?
Poison, I see, hath been his timeless end.
O churl! drunk all, and left no friendly drop
To help me after? I will kiss thy lips.
Haply some poison yet doth hang on them
To make me die with a restorative. [*Kisses him.*]
Thy lips are warm!

Chief Watch [*Within.*] Lead, boy. Which way?
JULIET Yea, noise? Then I'll be brief. O happy dagger!
[*Snatches Romeo's dagger.*]
This is thy sheath; there rust, and let me die.
[*She stabs herself and falls on Romeo's body.*]
[*Enter Paris's Boy and Watch.*]

Boy This is the place. There where the torch doth burn.
Chief Watch The ground is bloody. Search about the churchyard.
Go, some of you; whoe'er you find attach.
[*Exeunt some of the Watch.*]
Pitiful sight! Here lies the County slain;
And Juliet bleeding, warm and newly dead,
Who here hath lain this two days buried.
Go, tell the Prince; run to the Capulets;
Raise up the Montagues; some others search.
[*Exeunt other of the Watch.*]
We see the ground whereon these woes do lie,
But the true ground of all these piteous woes
We cannot without circumstance descry.
[*Enter some of the Watch, with Romeo's Man Balthasar.*]

罗密欧与朱丽叶
ROMEO AND JULIET

一只杯子,紧紧地握住在我的忠心的爱人的手里?我知道了,一定是毒药结果了他的生命。唉,冤家!你一起喝干了,不留下一滴给我吗?我要吻着你的嘴唇,也许这上面还留着一些毒液,可以让我当作兴奋剂服下而死去。(吻罗密欧)你的嘴唇还是温暖的!

巡丁甲　(在内)孩子,带路;在哪一个方向?

朱丽叶　啊,人声吗?那么我必须快一点了结。啊,好刀子!(攫住罗密欧的匕首)这就是你的鞘子;(以匕首自刺)你插了进去,让我死了吧。(扑在罗密欧身上死去)

　　　　(巡丁及帕里斯侍童上)

侍　童　就是这儿,那火把亮着的地方。

巡丁甲　地上都是血;你们几个人去把墓地四周搜查一下,看见什么人就抓起来。(若干巡丁下)好惨!伯爵被人杀了躺在这儿,朱丽叶胸口流着血,身上还是热热的好像死得不久,虽然她已经葬在这里两天了。去,报告亲王,通知凯普莱特家里,再去把蒙太古家里的人也叫醒了,剩下的人到各处搜搜。(若干巡丁续下)我们看见这些惨事发生在这个地方,可是在没有得到人证以前,却无法明了这些惨事的真相。

　　　　(若干巡丁率鲍尔萨泽上)

Second Watch	Here's Romeo's man. We found him in the churchyard.
Chief Watch	Hold him in safety till the Prince come hither.
	[*Enter Friar Laurence and another Watchman.*]
Third Watch	Here is a friar that trembles, sighs, and weeps.
	We took this mattock and this spade from him
	As he was coming from this churchyard side.
Chief Watch	A great suspicion! Stay the friar too.
	[*Enter the Prince and Attendants.*]
Prince	What misadventure is so early up,
	That calls our person from our morning rest?
	[*Enter Capulet and his wife with others.*]
CAPULET	What should it be, that is so shriek abroad?
Wife	The people in the street cry 'Remeo',
	Some 'Juliet', and some 'Paris'; and all run
	With open outcry, toward our monument.
Prince	What fear is this which startles in our ears?
Chief WATCH	Sovereign, here lies the County Paris slain;
	And Romeo dead; and Juliet, dead before,
	Warm and new kill'd.
Prince	Search, seek and know how this foul murder comes.
Chief Watch	Here is a friar, and slaughter'd Remeo's man,
	With instruments upon them fit to open
	These dead men's tombs.
CAPULET	O heavens! O wife, look how our daughter bleeds!
	This dagger hath mista'en, for, lo his house
	Is empty on the back of Montague,
	And it missheathed in my daughter's bosom!
Wife	O me! this sight of death is as a bell
	That warns my old age to a sepulchre.

罗密欧与朱丽叶
ROMEO AND JULIET

巡丁乙　这是罗密欧的仆人；我们看见他躲在墓地里。

巡丁甲　把他好生看押起来，等亲王来审问。

（若干巡丁率劳伦斯神父上）

巡丁丙　我们看见这个教士从墓地旁边跑出来，神色慌张，一边叹气一边流泪，他手里还拿着锄头铁锹，都给我们拿下来了。

巡丁甲　他有很重大的嫌疑；把这教士也看押起来。

（亲王及侍从上）

亲王　什么祸事在这样早的时候发生，打断了我的清晨的安睡？

（凯普莱特、凯普莱特夫人及余人等上）

凯普莱特　外边这样乱叫乱喊，是怎么一回事？

凯普莱特夫人　街上的人们有的喊着罗密欧，有的喊着朱丽叶，有的喊着帕里斯；大家沸沸扬扬地向我们家里的坟上奔去。

亲王　这么许多人为什么发出这样惊人的叫喊？

巡丁甲　王爷，帕里斯伯爵被人杀死了躺在这儿；罗密欧也死了；已经死了两天的朱丽叶，身上还热着，又被人重新杀死了。

亲王　用心搜寻，把这场万恶的杀人命案的真相调查出来。

巡丁甲　这儿有一个教士，还有一个被杀的罗密欧的仆人，他们都拿着掘墓的器具。

凯普莱特　天啊！——啊，妻子！瞧我们的女儿流着这么多的血！这把刀弄错了地位了！瞧，它的空鞘子还在蒙太古家小子的背上，它却插进了我的女儿的胸前！

凯普莱特夫人　哎哟！这些死的惨象就像惊心动魄的钟声，警告我这风烛残年，快要不久于人世了。

[*Enter Montague and others.*]

Prince Come, Montague, for thou art early up
To see thy son and heir more early down.

MONTAGUE Alas, my liege, my wife is dead to-night!
Grief of my son's exile hath stopp'd her breath.
What further woe conspires against mine age?

Prince Look, and thou shalt see.

MONTAGUE O thou untaught! what manners is in this,
To press before thy father to a grave?

Prince Seal up the mouth of outrage for a while,
Till we can clear these ambiguities
And know their spring, their head, their true descent;
And then will I be general of your woes
And lead you even to death. Meantime forbear,
And let mischance be slave to patience.
Bring forth the parties of suspicion.

Friar I am the greatest, able to do least,
Yet most suspected, as the time and place
Doth make against me, of this direful murther;
And here I stand, both to impeach and purge
Myself condemned and myself excus'd.

Prince Then say at once what thou dost know in this.

Friar I will be brief, for my short date of breath
Is not so long as is a tedious tale.
Romeo, there dead, was husband to that Juliet;
And she, there dead, that Romeo's faithful wife.
I married them; and their stol'n marriage day
Was Tybalt's doomsday, whose untimely death
Banish'd the new-made bridegroom from this city;

（蒙太古及余人等上）

亲　　　王　来，蒙太古，你起来虽然很早，可是你的儿子倒下得更早。

蒙 太 古　唉！殿下，我的妻子因为悲伤小儿的远逐，已经在昨天晚上去世了；还有什么祸事要来跟我这老头子作对呢？

亲　　　王　瞧吧，你就可以看见。

蒙 太 古　啊，你这不孝的东西！你怎么可以抢在你父亲的前面，自己先钻到坟墓里去呢？

亲　　　王　暂时停止你们的悲恸，让我把这些可疑的事实审问明白，知道了详细的原委以后，再来领导你们放声一哭吧；也许我的悲哀还要远远胜过你们呢！——把嫌疑犯带上来。

劳 伦 斯　时间和地点都可以作不利于我的证人；在这场悲惨的血案中，我虽然是一个能力最薄弱的人，但却是嫌疑最重的人。我现在站在殿下的面前，一方面要供认我自己的罪过，一方面也要为我自己辩解。

亲　　　王　那么快把你所知道的一切说出来。

劳 伦 斯　我要把经过的情形尽量简单地叙述出来，因为我的短促的残生还不及一段冗烦的故事那么长。死了的罗密欧是死了的朱丽叶的丈夫，她是罗密欧的忠心的妻子，他们的婚礼是由我主持的。就在他们秘密结婚的那天，提伯尔特死于非命，这位才做新郎的人也从这城里被

For whom, and not for Tybalt, Juliet pin'd.
You, to remove that siege of grief from her,
Betroth'd and would have married her perforce
To County Paris. Then comes she to me
And with wild looks bid me devise some mean
To rid her from this second marriage,
Or in my cell there would she kill herself.
Then gave I her (so tutored by my art)
A sleeping potion; which so took effect
As I intended, for it wrought on her
The form of death. Meantime I writ to Romeo
That he should hither come as this dire night
To help to take her from her borrowed grave,
Being the time the potion's force should cease.
But he which bore my letter, Friar John,
Was stay'd by accident, and yesternight
Return'd my letter back. Then all alone
At the prefixed hour of her waking
Came I to take her from her kindred's vault;
Meaning to keep her closely at my cell
Till I conveniently could send to Romeo.
But when I came, some minute ere the time
Of her awaking, here untimely lay
The noble Paris and true Romeo dead.
She wakes; and I entreated her come forth
And bear this work of heaven with patience;
But then a noise did scare me from the tomb,
And she, too desperate, would not go with me,
But, as it seems, did violence on herself.

罗密欧与朱丽叶
ROMEO AND JULIET

放逐出去；朱丽叶是为了他，不是为了提伯尔特，才那样伤心憔悴。你们因为要替她解除烦恼，把她许婚给帕里斯伯爵，还要强迫她嫁给他，她就跑来见我，神色慌张地要我替她想个办法避免这第二次的结婚，否则她要在我的寺院里自杀。所以我就根据我的医药方面的学识，给她一服安眠的药水；它果然发生了我所预期的效力，她一服下去就像死了一样昏沉过去。同时我写信给罗密欧，叫他就在这一个悲惨的晚上到这儿来，帮助把她搬出她寄寓的坟墓，因为药性一到时候便会过去。可是替我带信的约翰神父却因遭到意外，不能脱身，昨天晚上才把我的信依然带了回来。那时我只好按照着预先算定她醒来的时间，一个人前去把她从她家族的墓茔里带出来，预备把她藏匿在我的寺院里，等有方便再去叫罗密欧来；不料我在她醒来以前几分钟到这儿来的时候，尊贵的帕里斯和忠诚的罗密欧已经双双惨死了。她一醒过来，我就请她出去，劝她安心忍受这一种出自天意的变故；可是那时我听见了纷纷的人声，吓得逃出了墓穴，她在万分绝望之中不肯跟我去，看样子她是自杀了。这是我所知道的

	All this I know, and to the marriage
	Her nurse is privy; and if aught in this
	Miscarried by my fault, let my old life
	Be sacrific'd, some hour before the time,
	Unto the rigour of severest law.
Prince	We still have known thee for a holy man.
	Where's Romeo's man? What can he say to this?
BALTHASAR	I brought my master news of Juliet's death;
	And then in post he came from Mantua
	To this same place, to this same monument.
	This letter he early bid me give his father,
	And threat'ned me with death, going in the vault,
	If I departed not and left him there.
Prince	Give me the letter. I will look on it.
	Where is the County's page that rais'd the watch?
	Sirrah, what made your master in this place?
Boy	He came with flowers to strew his lady's grave;
	And bid me stand aloof, and so I did.
	Anon comes one with light to ope the tomb;
	And by-and-by my master drew on him;
	And then I ran away to call the watch.
Prince	This letter doth make good the friar's words,
	Their course of love, the tidings of her death;
	And here he writes that he did buy a poison
	Of a poor pothecary, and therewithal
	Came to this vault to die, and lie with Juliet.
	Where be these enemies? Capulet, Montague,
	See what a scourge is laid upon your hate,
	That heaven finds means to kill your joys with love!

一切，至于他们两人的结婚，那么她的乳母也是耳闻的。要是这一场不幸的惨祸，是由我的疏忽所造成，那么我这条老命愿受最严厉的法律的制裁，请您让它提早几点钟牺牲了吧。

亲　　王　我一向知道你是一个道行高尚的人。罗密欧的仆人呢？他有什么话说？

鲍尔萨泽　我把朱丽叶的死讯通知了我的主人，因此他从曼图亚急急地赶到这里，到了这座坟茔的前面。这封信他叫我一早送去给我家老爷；当他走进墓穴里的时候，他还恐吓我，说要是我不离开他赶快走开，他就要杀死我。

亲　　王　把那封信给我，我要看看。叫巡丁来的那个伯爵的侍童呢？喂，你的主人到这地方来做什么？

侍　　童　他带了花来散在他夫人的坟上，他叫我站得远远的，我就听他的话；不一会儿工夫，来了一个拿着火把的人把坟墓打开了。后来我的主人就拔剑跟他打了起来，我就奔去叫巡丁。

亲　　王　这封信证实了这个神父的话，讲起他们恋爱的经过和她的去世的消息；他还说他从一个穷苦的卖药人手里买到一种毒药，要把它带到墓穴里来准备和朱丽叶长眠在一起。这两家仇人在哪里？——凯普莱特！蒙太古！瞧你们的仇恨已经受到了多大的惩罚，上天借手于爱情，夺去了你们心爱的人；我为了忽视你们的争执，

	And I, for winking at your discords too,
	Have lost a brace of kinsmen. All are punish'd.
CAPULET	O brother Montague, give me thy hand.
	This is my daughter's jointure, for no more
	Can I demand.
MONTAGUE	But I can give thee more;
	For I will raise her Statue in pure gold,
	That whiles Verona by that name is known,
	There shall no figure at such rate be set
	As that of true and faithful Juliet.
CAPULET	As rich shall Romeo's by his lady's lie —
	Poor sacrifices of our enmity!
Prince	A glooming peace this morning with it brings.
	The sun for sorrow will not show his head.
	Go hence, to have more talk of these sad things;
	Some shall be pardon'd, and some punished;
	For never was a story of more woe
	Than this of Juliet and her Romeo.
	[*Exeunt.*]

	也已经丧失了一双亲戚,大家都受到惩罚了。
凯普莱特	啊,蒙太古大哥!把你的手给我;这就是你给我女儿的一份聘礼,我不能再作更大的要求了。
蒙 太 古	但是我可以给你更多的;我要用纯金替她铸一座像,只要维罗纳一天不改变它的名称,任何塑像都不会比忠贞的朱丽叶那一座更为卓越。
凯普莱特	罗密欧也要有一座同样富丽的金像卧在他情人的身旁,这两个在我们的仇恨下惨遭牺牲的可怜的人儿!
亲 王	清晨带来了凄凉的和解, 太阳也惨得在云中躲闪。 大家先回去发几声感慨, 该恕的、该罚的再听宣判。 古往今来多少离合悲欢, 谁曾见这样的哀怨辛酸!(同下)